INVITING THE MYSTIC, SUPPORTING THE PROPHET

Inviting the Mystic, Supporting the Prophet

An Introduction to Spiritual Direction

Katherine Marie Dyckman, S.N.J.M.
L. Patrick Carroll, S.J.

PAULIST PRESS
New York/Ramsey

Library of Congress
Catalog Card Number: 81-80053

ISBN: 0-8091-2378-9

Published by Paulist Press
545 Island Road, Ramsey, N.J. 07446

Printed and bound in the
United States of America

CONTENTS

FOREWORD ix

INTRODUCTION 1

1 FAITHING 7

2 CONTEMPORARY SPIRITUALITY 15

3 DEFINING SPIRITUAL DIRECTION 20

4 PRESUPPOSITIONS OF THE DIRECTOR 31

5 PRESUPPOSITIONS ABOUT PRAYER 42

6 PROBLEMS IN PRAYER 51

7 PRAYING THROUGH THE DESERT 61

8 PRAYERFUL DECISION MAKING 70

9 MYSTICS AND PROPHETS 77

APPENDIX 87

SELECTED BIBLIOGRAPHY 90

to Marie and Dug
Zelda, Tally and Edith

FOREWORD

"Faith without works is dead." This is the blunt answer given by the Apostle James to the perennial question about the relationship between belief and deeds. Today, we might phrase the question differently. We might ask about the relationship between faith and justice, prayer and action, spirituality and social commitment. But the answer is still the same. Faith without works is dead.

How, then, do we grow in the faith that does justice? It seems to me that at issue here is not how people of action can be led to deepen their faith. Nor is it how praying people can be led to action. Rather, how can anyone be led to an authentic encounter with Jesus, Lord of History, in his mission? How and where do we meet the historical Jesus who builds his Reign today in our world?

This meeting with Jesus, being with him, in order to participate in his mission, to be sent out, is central to the basic evangelical experience of call. In Mark 3:14, we learn that Jesus called his disciples and told them: "I have chosen you to be with me; I will also send you out to preach and you will have authority to drive out demons" (*Good News* version). To be close to Jesus and to be moving out in service of others: this is the call.

But we all know that this meeting and following of Jesus is neither automatic nor easy, especially for the busy person of today. This is true whether one is the mother of a family or a single person, a priest or a religious, a sales representative or a doctor. To be honest, we also have to admit that much of the spiritual advice offered to these busy people today tends to be highly individualistic, narrowly personalistic. The social consequences of being with Jesus—i.e., being sent out by and with him in mission—are not always stressed in books on prayer and in experiences of spiritual direction. Yet the very climate of social change today seriously challenges this personalistic approach.

"More and more, in all our surroundings, we hear pleas for help in developing that personal relationship with the Lord that allows us, frees us, to be and to do justice with and for others." In this way, Katherine Dyckman and Pat Carroll describe the challenge they have experienced in their ministry. Developing a response to these pleas is the task which the authors have set for themselves in this study. They are convinced that inviting the prophet and supporting the mystic are two aspects of the same project: assisting the person to meet Jesus.

Their basic insight, it seems to me, is that all prayer and spiritual direction is focused on *response*. They contend that authentic prayer leads the individual person "to respond to Christ in the given historical cultural moment." Each responds in a unique way, to unique situations in which he or she finds the Lord calling His people. But all respond outside themselves in service. Each mystic becomes a prophet.

In the struggle to respond in a fashion which combines the qualities of mystic and prophet, we come to know more deeply the complexity of our own existence. Let me suggest here three areas which for me must be taken seriously if we are to have a social spirituality which promotes the integration of faith and justice.

First, for the past several years, I have been helped to understand the necessity of a social dimension to spirituality by a particular way of looking at the levels of my human existence. (Thomas Clarke, S.J., and I first developed this theme in 1974 in articles in SOUNDINGS.) Each of us exist at three levels; we live and move and have our being in three spheres of reality. There is the *intrapersonal* level of existence, where

I am an individual, unique, different from all others, along before my Creator. But there is also the *interpersonal* level of existence, in which I exist in and through relationships with other persons. These relationships, profound or superficial, shape my life and embody my being. Beyond these two, however, there is a third level of existence, the *public* level. Here I exist in the institutions, the social structures, the public processes of society around me—business, law, government, education, church, family, etc. I am necessarily a part of these institutions and structures. Literally, I cannot be a "private person" and live a full existence.

What this says to me as one struggling to grow as a person of faith is that just as interpersonal relationships cannot be abstracted from in prayer or direction, neither can my public involvement or stance be neglected. I cannot "get myself together" *first* at an intrapersonal (very individualistic) level, simply because I do not exist first—or at any other moment, for that matter—at only this level. Sensitivity to political events such as war, social ills such as racism and sexism, or economic crises such as unemployment is not something optional in my spiritual growth. Such sensitivity is basic to my full Christian existence.

Second, I am becoming more convinced that the "faith and culture" linkage needs to be emphasized in any discussion of prayer and direction. "Inculturation" is one of the themes-of-the-moment in religious circles. It means that we must recognize that faith, to be alive, has to take form within the concrete confines of a specific culture. Yet it is never fully captured by that culture, but must be free to critique and challenge. Hence prayer that nourishes the life of faith must be sensitive to cultural influences.

Simply to speak of the United States milieu with which I am most familiar, there is a powerful shaping of religious experience by the cultural factors and vehicles which touch every aspect of our lives—e.g., the spirit of competition, the style of the media, the pull of consumerism, the impact of affluence, the character of pluralism. To be immersed daily in the world of television images (especially those of advertisements), for instance, has tremendous consequences for an imagination which would envision Jesus in his mission today. A discernment of the positive and negative influences of culture is, therefore, crucial to growth in a life which responds to Christ in the challenges of everyday life.

Third, in a way which sometimes surprises me I have come to believe that *commitment* is prior to *intimacy*. One must make an option, take a stand, before everything is clear. Specifically, the knowledge of Jesus in his mission comes primarily from following him in his mission. The Latin American theologian Jon Sobrino emphasizes this point when he speaks of the need to be part of the building of the Kingdom if one is ever to come to know the Lord. This may appear paradoxical. Can I love someone I do not know? Of course not. But love begets knowledge. Commitment to the Lord in his mission is itself a source of becoming intimately acquainted with him as a person.

But what does it mean to follow Jesus in the work of the Reign? It means identifying with his struggle for establishing that sisterhood and brotherhood which is a consequence of our experiencing daughtership and sonship of "Abba," the loving Mother-Father who has created us. People relate as sisters and brothers when the conditions of justice and peace—the social manifestation of the works of faith—are present. For this reason, prayer and direction can never be purely privatistic or socially unconcerned if their goal is to move us toward a knowledge and following of Jesus.

The thrust of Katherine and Pat's study is in the direction of promoting these three areas of social spirituality, namely, the recognition of our public existence, the sensitivity to cultural influences on faith, and the following of Jesus as a prerequisite to knowledge of him. There are, of course, other themes which, while not explicitly developed by the authors in this study, should suggest themselves to the reader as worthy of further exploration.

For example, how important is it that persons who direct others should themselves be enriched by social experiences of poverty, injustice and cultural conflict? Many religious communities are designing formation experiences—for novices as well as for older religious—which emphasize these social experiences. Moreover, how sensitive should a director be to the movements of "social desolation" and "social consolation" within an individual—i.e., the stirrings which are consequences of the socio-economic and political environment within which a person is located? A feeling of fear and helplessness, for instance, in the face of nuclear arms race can affect the prayer of a sensitive person just as much as personal problems of poor self-image. Furthermore, what is the relationship of life-style to prayer? For instance, is there an impact of simpler surroundings such as in a retreat house on the openness of a retreatant to hear the call of the poor? These and other themes suggest themselves once we begin probing the implications of a social dimension in everything we say about prayer and direction.

Discussion of mystics and prophets, then, must ultimately return to a focus on the one who, joined mystically to "Abba," was the prophetic "person for others" in laying down his life in service. Jesus exemplified the integration of the qualities spoken of in the pages which follow. Certainly the test for authentic encounter with Jesus is always: what difference does it make in my life of service? Is my faith alive with the works of justice?

Peter J. Henriot, S.J.
Center of Concern
Washington, D.C.
February 27, 1981

INTRODUCTION

> *Thanks be to God who, wherever he goes, makes us, in Christ, partners of his triumph, and through us is spreading the knowledge of himself, like a sweet smell everywhere. We are Christ's incense to God for those who are being saved and those who are not; for the last the sweet smell of death that leads to death, for the first the sweet smell of life that leads to life (2 Cor. 2:14–16).*

The telephone rings. "I am looking for a spiritual director. I've called several priests and none of them is available. Two of them referred me to you. Can you take some time to talk with me on some kind of regular basis about my relationship with God, my prayer, in fact, my whole life?"

We wait, sigh, look at our schedule and respond—sometimes with a "yes," sometimes with a "no," never with complete comfort. Something needs to be done. There simply must be more people who can undertake this kind of relationship. It is so necessary, so frequently asked for, so often seemingly unobtainable.

This dilemma is the subject of this book.

Despite a tremendous resurgence of interest in prayer and spirituality within the Roman Catholic Church the past several years, few books have dealt with the subject of spiritual direction. Yet the journey of faith is a journey shared. We do not, cannot travel alone. Though books can inspire, encourage, or freshen the spirit, it is often in dialogue with another that one best grows in the personal meeting with the Lord.

We are convinced that many more of us can be the kind of companions to others that can facilitate this growth. Both of us have been involved in this kind of work in our separate ministries for years: Sr. Katherine Dyckman as a director of formation within her Holy Names community, with seminarians and with others for the past ten years; Fr. Pat Carroll as an assistant to the novice master in his Jesuit community, as religious superior of a high school community, and as pastor of a parish. Three years ago the two of us returned from a year of working with religious in Lesotho, South Africa, with the germ of an idea. Each of us had experienced far more people requesting personal direction than we were able to imagine handling. Each of us believed that there existed within all types of communities in the Church the resources to provide for their own members. What if, we questioned, we were to offer help to parish and other community-based people to be directors, guides, companions within their own milieu? For the past two years we have offered a variety of seminars to people in parishes, in the cursillo movement, in charismatic prayer groups, in hospital ministry, and in religious communities, and to a variety of other gatherings of Christian peoples. This book represents the outgrowth of those classes, enriched by the insights, comments, criticisms and experiences of the participants in those seminars.

We began to offer this series to lay people, sisters and priests with the theory that many people look for someone to be with them in their prayer and their lives of faith in general, yet few feel qualified to do so. Yet at the same time many people are talking about their faith life and their prayer to each other in less formal and structured ways. Unlike the caller in the initial paragraph of this chapter, the direction relationship often begins with someone asking for a book on prayer, wondering where to make a retreat, or simply discussing life over an afternoon beer.

People tend to turn to priests as experts in this area, but priests never seem to have time, or, if the truth be spoken, the confidence to undertake the task. What seems needed at every level of the Church is the confidence of many to become the companions to others, using their gifts of nature and grace. And also needed is the opportunity to continue to do so with increasing confidence.

Another realization that led us to begin to try to help form "spiritual directors" revolves around the phenomenon that many call "burn out." For the past ten years we have been invited, indeed challenged by the Church to engage in the transformation of the social order. The most responsive among us took up that challenge and went into the fray. Sadly, the most immediate to respond to the deepest call of the Church found themselves frequently exhausted and discouraged long before the social order found itself transformed. In a typical city parish many of the leaders of ten years ago are no longer present and active in the Church community. If they attend Mass at all, they do so at a distance and without involvement. The Church failed to nourish their enthusiasm which either died or was fed at some other table.

Concretely, the Church calls us to the *faith* that *does justice,* but so often people entered into the justice arena without sufficient help in the arena of faith, help that would nourish the continuance of the struggle. For many, the Church, ultimately Jesus himself and the kingdom of the Father, became irrelevant to their sense of the struggle for the very real and tangible needs of oppressed people.

We became convinced of the need to provide support systems, faith systems to kindle nourishment for those who try to *do,* not just theoretically *believe,* Christianity. The intrinsic relationship between faith and justice invites the response of all believers. That relationship, as we specifically choose to approach it, is not between the *notion* of faith and the *notion* of justice, but between the interpersonal relationship of faith and the doing of justice, the accomplishment of it. It is a dynamic relationship, for faith is a "doing of the truth," not just a "holding of the truth." Because we are loved, we love.

More and more, in all our surroundings, we hear pleas for help in developing that personal relationship with the Lord that allows us, frees us, to be and to do justice with and for others. Those lay, clerical, and vowed persons most deeply involved in building the kingdom of God in the external order need all the guidance, direction, support and companionship that the Church can provide for the building of that kingdom in their hearts.

There is a tremendous diversity in "doing justice." Our specific concern involves the formation of leaders, enablers, companions who can support the underlying faith relationship.

That relationship both motivates and allows Christians to see the deeper meaning of the history which they fashion with their own hands in communion with other persons and with God.

We offer these reflections on the role of spiritual director to encourage those already involved in the task, to build upon the natural gifts of those people who feel called to begin, to increase the number of hearts willing to hear in this way, and, in all of this, to help the Church to be Church, not for itself, but for others.

We will not try to detail exactly how another can go about the task of direction, so much as to suggest the spirit that can underpin the dialogue, the attitudes the director brings into the dialogue, and some of the tools that may help that dialogue to flow.

Our expectations are modest. We hope to help the reader to become a bit more comfortable and competent in leading others in prayer and in the whole of their life of faith. We consider ourselves leaders, but not "gurus," experts, or even "professionals" in spirituality. Rather, we are praying, seeking people trying to talk with some understanding to others like ourselves. We offer our reflections to those who are themselves trying to pray, to share the fruits and struggles of that prayer and the lives that result from that prayer with others. We offer these reflections to those open to listening to the marvelous stories of other fellow Christian searchers.

In the course of this book we will open up only introductory topics, areas that will need pursuance as expertise deepens. Our initial chapter raises the question of faith as a developing, maturing reality, and the dynamic through which one ordinarily passes in the journey. Then we spend considerable time redefining both terms of our central subject: "Spiritual" and "Direction." Following this redefinition, we discuss our own presuppositions about both "directing" and "praying," the theoretical framework that we bring into any relationship.

Although there are a thousand books on prayer, we will include a treatment of prayer, faith life, thresholds to prayer, and some "techniques" to get started, or restarted, in the practice of prayer. Because prayer admits to "ups" and "downs," we treat some times that need special attention (how to start, what to do when things bog down, times of critical decision making, and the important area of quiet, passive, or dark contemplation).

The book ends with an effort to return where we began, with an indication of the inherent connection between prayer and life, contemplation and action, faith and justice.

Join us, then, in the journey.

As you read these pages, we invite you to constantly listen to your own story, and the story of others, to test our words and see if they ring true. To be helpful, this book needs to have its margins filled with your jottings, your experiences, your awareness of the experience of others. The book hopefully expects that you are talking about your own life of faith with others, and they are talking with you about theirs. It is our hope, then, that as you read this essay in spiritual direction, you are at the same time, in formal or informal ways, both directing and being directed yourself.

The uniqueness of the journey which we begin to examine in Chapter 1 reveals helpful discoveries of the recent years in our renewing Church. We are not all walking lock-step toward a uni-faceted God. A variety of gifts all contribute to a single, amazingly complex and beautiful body. Spirituality amazes by the many colors of its coat. We can share some of our experience, but your reading will be deeply aided by the continued paralleling of your own.

1 FAITHING

I do not consider myself to have arrived spiritually, nor do I consider myself already perfect. But I keep on going, grasping ever more firmly that purpose for which Christ Jesus grasped (overtook) me (Phil. 3:12).

A priest friend of ours responds somewhat originally to the common and understandable lament of parents who say, "I think my children are losing their faith." He responds, "Perhaps they are only losing your faith and discovering their own." Faith is a journey with many roads, stages and paths—a journey we journey with others.

It seems appropriate to begin our discussion of walking with others in faith by reflecting on our own personal journey, what we have to share with others. All of us are pilgrims on the way, whether we are twenty-five, or seventy-five. Life is a continuous call to change, to grow, to become in Christ. John Henry Cardinal Newman challenged a static view of Christian adulthood: "To live is to change; to be perfect is to have changed often." We speak of the paradox of the "already" and the "not yet," the ambiguity of both being mature and being called to grow, the deeply Christian reality of being both saved and yet sinner.

The contemporary work of James Fowler of Emory University on the stages of faith development complements Newman's realization that faith is a verb, a process, not a static reality.[1] We do not just "have faith." We *become* trusting, believing, "faithing" people as we wrestle with the givenness and crises of our lives. We are not finally married on our wedding day or fully priests at ordination; we *become* who God calls us to be. So baptism is a stage of the faith process, neither the beginning nor the end.

The personal change of central concern in Christianity from its very inception has been conversion/metanoia, the radical transformation in Christ.[2] Conversion is not a matter of prevailing arguments, of changing from one belief system to another, but a matter, rather, of our personal surrender to a personal, living God. This is what faith is all about.[3] A change from one belief system to another may or may not be a real conversion experience. Contemporary Catholics, feeling that the Church has abandoned its rules and regulations and missing the security that those boundaries used to provide, do not really change the depth of faith by becoming Mormons because of the clarity of their religious practice. They simply change the belief system, but do not grow or deepen in faith.

William Johnston, in *The Inner Eye of Love,* relying on Bernard Lonergan, draws a necessary distinction between faith and belief:

> It is possible to distinguish between a superstructure which I shall call *belief* and an infrastructure which I shall call *faith.* The superstructure (belief) is the outer word, the outer revelation, the word spoken in history and conditioned by culture. The infrastructure (faith) on the other hand is the interior word, the word spoken to the heart, the inner revelation.[4]

From our own ministries, we know that people who profess no particular belief system often harbor deep faith within them without knowing, much less attempting to articulate it. Those whom we welcome into our tradition are often persons of profound faith who have for the first time had that phenomenon come to conscious awareness in their lives. So, also, cradle Catholics sometimes experience a growth in the conscious awareness of the connection between a faith life that has grown in them unconsciously and the forms of religion that they had always "practiced."

So by *faith* we mean not just mental assent to the content/propositions of faith, or one phenomenon among others, but the central phenomenon in one's life—better, a central relationship that gives meaning to one's life and allows one to perceive reality and to interpret one's experiences in the light of that relationship. To "faith" is to hand over the direction of one's journey to another, to yield up what Sam Keen calls "the illusion of control"[5] to someone who is essentially beyond our control, over whom we have no power. To "faith" is to allow oneself to be overtaken by God in the way Paul was, and to do so many times: "I do not consider myself to have arrived spiritually nor do I consider myself already perfect. But I keep on going, grasping ever more firmly that purpose for which Christ Jesus grasped (overtook) me" (Phil 3:12).

Each of our journeys is unique insofar as our relationship with God is unique, and yet there are similarities in the pattern of faith moving toward God. Common threads run through the lives of Augustine, Teresa of Avila, Thomas Merton, of those persons who today enter our faith communities, of ourselves, and even of Jesus himself.[6] In all of these journeys, to one degree or another, there are the common elements of (a) conversion, (b) a struggle to internalize and act on that conversion experience, (c) a call to integrity, (d) a call to reality, and (e) a call to radicality. These elements emerge regardless of differing eras, cultures, theologies, life-styles, or ministries.

The first thing in common is the experience of *conversion* (as we have described above). Conversion is the hallmark of genuine faith development, but is possible only when we are in relationship to another because it implies letting go and surrendering to another in love. We cannot even begin to have a sense of infidelity or unfaithfulness until we discover what love is and what it is to love. If we have not yet tasted or seen or felt something of the love of God and others, we cannot sin because sin, infidelity, is a correlative to love.

We have described faith primarily as relationship. Any love relationship challenges us to greater honesty and transparency, to awareness of those areas of our lives where we hold back or refuse to face ourselves or to let others see us as we are. To really love others means to become progressively more vulnerable to them, to risk letting them see us in the bad times as well as the good, trusting that they will still love us. This is essentially what we mean by conversion/metanoia. Real conversion is centered on God; it results from a deeper turning toward him rather than a closer inspection of ourselves.

But this very turning calls us away from our middle-class values, our self-rightousness, our complacency, or from a life ruled by fear. Conversion, at its root, is not the action performed but the source of that action, the experience of being loved.

We are converted many times, and this endless series of large and small conversions, inner revolutions, leads to our growth in Christ. Faith is really the readiness to enter more deeply into this process of letting God shape us, stretch us and lead us to new depths of trust, love and freedom, by changing our image of him, of ourselves, and of reality. So Mother Teresa leaves her community to start a whole new life on the streets of Calcutta. Charles de Foucauld spends twenty years in the desert without a single convert. Everything is sold for the pearl of great price because God turns us around by the intense experience of love.

The second common element that marks the journey is *struggle.* Some conversion experiences are obviously more key than others. Struggle often ensues in actualizing the experience, in "owning" it, in acting on it. Everything in our society seems to lead us to mistrust our experiences of God, to deny or water them down. We question the validity of the invitation, discount the fact that *we* can have religious experience, worry about what others will think, and, generally, struggle with the call to change. Prayer becomes a tug-of-war. Jacob's wrestling with the Angel/God (Gen. 32:23–29) becomes an archetype for spiritual and human growth, a battle, not with God, but with the false self that seeks control, and this is precisely what faith counters.

Without expanding on each part it may be helpful to point out that Elisabeth Kübler-Ross' stages of dying are the same that one is likely to grow through in the death-struggle that growth in faith demands: denial, anger, bargaining, depression, and, finally, acceptance.

The deeper surrendering called forth in the struggle of conversion also facilitates a *call to integrity,* to be wholly who God calls us to be, to become our real and best selves. This third common element is not a seeking of self-fulfillment, but a summons to quit playing games, to let our interior, private selves become congruent with our exterior, public selves. In religious terms, this integrating is not just for ourselves, so that we feel "together," but precisely so that we can best *do* for others. The Christian paradox is that this does indeed lead to self-fulfillment. This integrity removes us from the temptation to continue trying to fool others, even though we know we cannot fool ourselves, cannot fool God.

The fourth element is a *call,* in some form or other, *into a deeper sense of reality.* We see events and people around us with new clarity. We become personally, deeply touched by the horror of world hunger, the absurdity and ambiguity of the Iranian and Afghanistan situations, the painful plight of boat people, the insanity of a tiny crippled child being shot by a sniper. There grows a dawning sense of the interconnectedness of all phases of our life as we put on the mind of Christ. We see the incongruence of fighting abortion but supporting the build-up of nuclear armaments, the inconsistency of combating racism while continuing to discriminate against women. The basic truths through which reality is filtered converge and narrow.

Finally, an authentic faith journey always leads to concern for others, to a *radicality of love,* in some form or other. We begin to see, to feel that a lack of concern for the world or an inability to bear the burden of others and to share in their suffering is a sign that we share neither the mind nor the heart of Christ. We realize that the highest form of love is not simply to love God but to share in his love for others. We no longer seek to love like Christ but to love with him, and in him and through him.

We will be returning to the dynamics of this journey in Chapter 9, but we must begin here to form a basis for reflection on our own journey if we would presume to walk with others.

The journey is often described as one of darkness (John of the Cross, *The Cloud of Unknowing,* and the entire apophatic school). It is so termed because we cannot lead, for we do not know where to go. Like Abraham, our father in faith, we followers go out in trust to a land we do not know, a land which God will show us. The darkness envelops because we, with our human intelligence, are incapable of penetrating God. The other can be reached and held close only by love. Knowledge of God (knowledge in the intimate, physical, biblical sense) is supraconceptual, beyond our concepts of him, and obtained only through the freely given gift of love. This is a kind of knowing by unknowing, this believing that a lack of consoling experience and a lack of knowledge in the cognitive sense can be the most real presence of God.

> If God is hidden, it is because he is out of the reach of our senses or imagination, even of our mental perceptions. . . . It is true that our reason can get at least some glimpse of his existence, and we learn even more about him through the revealed Scripture; yet he remains always beyond any conceptual knowledge that man can have of him.[6]

The same is true in a deep human relationship where lovers do not *know* each other because they can give detailed descriptions of physical or personal traits but because they love, intuit, grasp the other by whom they have been grasped.

The effect of faith is that we are no longer firmly based within ourselves, a fact that often brings with it uncertainty and doubt. This is only one of the reasons why *faith is impossible in isolation from others.* We recall a letter from a former student, a young married man, in which he poignantly described his own struggle with the darkness of the journey. He said that he could no longer bear the pain of being a Christian, that he had sincerely prayed to God and found only silence. He made the decision never to become involved with God like that again because the hurt was so great. He was going to go back to what he had been before, someone well thought of by others, living a decent life, and being satisfied with his own self-respect. With such a person there is no point developing counter-arguments. No amount of calculated reasoning will ease his darkness or strengthen him to carry on with the apparently empty search. He did not need answers or arguments. What he needed and wanted, even as he denied the desire for it, was the presence of one who had been there before, who had doubted and struggled but had somehow stumbled on.

In closing this section, let us look for a moment at the deepest basis for our own faith, Jesus. But let us look at Jesus for a moment not as the object of our faith, but as the *man of faith.* He taught, not only in parables, but by his whole life and ministry, how he made the journey himself. Jesus recognized the battle between the forces of light and darkness as they occurred in his own person. The accounts of his temptations in the desert, stylized as they are, still capture the wrestling of his own spirit to trust blindly in the Father, to throw himself unreservedly on the Father's love and saving power, rather than to trust in his own power and not accept the risk of total destruction. This decision, which began his ministry, was painfully tested many times, but is especially seen as the final decisive test in the agony in the garden that precedes his death and resurrection.

The "lust for certitude" that we sometimes see in ourselves and criticize in others is not the mind and heart of Christ. It is a subtle, or not so subtle, form of religious fundamentalism, one that sees religion as the answer to life's questions rather than unveiling a Person who allows us to live with the questions. Religion always offers the temptation to define salvation in terms of practices, external observances of the law, the nine first Fridays, the stations of the cross, or a magic three Hail Marys before retiring. In themselves these are admirable, but they can become a way of certainty, of earning salvation, a substitute for authentic faith, another attempt to control my life, and the kind of legalism which Jesus consistently decried. They stand in the way of the surrendering faith that risks all as Jesus did.

In the course of his life, Jesus recognized that his ability to minister and to proclaim salvation to others was based on his willingness to acknowledge and engage in his own struggle for salvation. In some way, the struggle of Jesus is everyone's struggle. He was faced with questions of identity and integrity with who he was called to be and what his mission truly was—

whatever might have been the messianic expectations of his day. And so are we! The great illusion of Christians engaged in any ministry, and so in the ministry of directing others, is to think that we can lead others into faith, lead others out of their various deserts and darknesses without having been there ourselves.

We can most help the people we would minister to as directors by loving them, challenging them, creating real faith communities with and for them, and especially by sharing with them our own weaknesses and fragility in making the journey. Then, together, we can face our difficulties with the expectation of faith that reveals the hidden potential of people and of life. This is what Jesus did, and what we are called to do.

NOTES

1. Read James Fowler's interesting discussion with Sam Keen in *Life Maps: Conversations on the Journey of Faith* (Waco, Texas: Word Books, 1978).
2. Evelyn E. Whitehead and James D. Whitehead, *Christian Life Patterns* (New York: Doubleday and Co., 1979), p. 34.
3. See Paul Tillich's classic *Dynamics of Faith* (New York: Harper and Row, 1957).
4. William Johnston, *The Inner Eye of Love* (San Francisco: Harper and Row, 1978), p. 68.
5. Sam Keen, *Life Maps,* p. 105.
6. Abhishiktananda (Fr. Henri Le Saux, O.S.B.), *Prayer* (Philadelphia: Westminster Press, 1972), p. 9.

2 CONTEMPORARY SPIRITUALITY

What does it profit a man to gain the whole world and suffer the loss of his soul? (Mt. 16:26, Douay-Rheims)

What then will a man gain if he wins the whole world and ruins his life? (Mt. 16:26, Jerusalem Bible)

Before we undertake to define what we mean by "spiritual direction," the term "spirituality" requires some close attention. Two quite divergent understandings of that word and that reality are operative. The first might be characterized by recalling Thomas a Kempis' famous line from *The Imitation of Christ,* "Everytime I go out into the world I come back less a monk." The second flows from the initial lines of the final document of Vatican II, *Gaudium et Spes:* "The joys and the hopes, the griefs and the anxieties of the men of this age, especially those who are poor or in any way afflicted, these too are the joys and hopes, the griefs and anxieties of the followers of Christ. . . . This community realizes that it is truly and intimately linked with mankind and its history."[1]

Since it is in today's church-world that we are to speak of directing others, we need to reflect on what constitutes contemporary spirituality. In the introductory chapters of his marvelous book, *On Becoming a Musical Mystical Bear,* Matthew Fox treats of "old" and "new" spiritually.[2] Using his reflections as a base, we suggest an examination of our own presuppositions about spirituality. The questions raised in this section will be developed more fully as we go along, but we here initiate a direction for our dialogue.

The revival of Scripture study and Scripture-based prayer involving a move back from a Greek to a Hebrew mentality underlies what we will term contemporary spirituality. In place of abstract, philosophical systems, and a highly intellectual approach to God, we seek to foster today a concrete, personal, divine-human interaction. Spirituality reaches beyond the neo-

Platonic thought and prayer patterns of third-century Christians (and many ever since) to recapture and make new the thought and prayer patterns of Jesus and his more Eastern, Hebraic companions. In this search the same words take on different meanings.

In the text from Matthew's Gospel quoted at the beginning of this chapter there may at first seem to be little difference between "ruins his life" and "suffers the loss of his soul" of earlier translations, but symptomatically the difference is profound and deep. A Greek, philosophic thought pattern speaks of a body-soul dualism, of saving "souls," of the "spirit" as that immaterial part of ourselves that is the *real* us. Scripture and its thought patterns equate spirit with "that which is life-giving," the whole of the human person as inclined to God, to life, to freedom. Thus the biblical concern is with the saving of life, of the whole human person, not just some airy, insubstantial part. Scripture speaks of resurrection of the body person, and that as something that is already going on now.

The kind of dichotomy that marked our not-too-distant past needs redirection if our "spiritual" direction is to be contemporary and Christianly valid. We are not concerned with the "spirit" of a person apart from the person, or the soul apart from the personality. If we believe that matter is evil, rather than God-made, holy, the very stuff of salvation, we will find it difficult to direct someone who is trying to grow in an incarnational, bodily, enfleshed Christ/Church.

Often the spirituality of our past, so easily caricatured in a Kempis, reflected this neo-Platonic disdain for the body and the negative elements of asceticism: the limiting of pleasure, the crushing of pride and lust, the killing of self-love, the mortification of the senses. But our Redeemer prayed that "joy may be in you, and your joy may be complete" (Jn. 15:11). The greatest mortification may be to accept and utilize for others all the gifts we have received. Christian spirituality then is concerned not with life-denying, but life-affirming: "I have come that you may have life and have it more abundantly" (Jn. 10:10).

As we talk with another, we are not trying to point to

a God who is out of this world, but to a God who has chosen to become immersed in this world. We do not hope to discover or create a sacred place where another may retreat from a secular world, but to enhance a vision which sees the entire order of things as sacred. As a priest friend is fond of saying: "I'm not trying to get to heaven. I'm just trying to get down to earth." That is where Jesus is, and where God is found. The world is not divided into sacred and profane, but all is gift, and the mission of Christ and of all of us is to become, as the Council indicated, the Church *in* the modern world.

As Thomas Merton puts it so well in *Contemplation in a World of Action:*

> Do we really choose between the world and Christ as between two conflicting realities absolutely opposed? Or do we choose Christ by choosing the world as it really is in him, and encountered in the ground of our own personal freedom and of our love? Do we really renounce ourselves and the world in order to find Christ, or do we renounce our alienated and false selves in order to choose our own deepest truth in choosing both the world and Christ at the same time? If the deepest ground of my being is love, then in that very love itself and nowhere else will I find myself, and the world, and my brother, and Christ. It is not a question of either-or but of all-in-one . . . of wholeness, wholeheartedness and unity . . . which finds the same ground of love in everything.[3]

Further, spirituality is not adequately described as building up my private relationship with God: a "Jesus and I" mentality. Perhaps the most radical renewed revelation of the Council is the participative dimension of our relationship with God who is pleased to save us not as individuals but as a people.

> It has pleased God, however, to make men holy and save them not merely as individuals without any mutual

> bonds, but by making them into a single people which acknowledges him in truth and serves him in holiness.[4]

A valid contemporary spirituality is, to some extent at least, a communal spirituality, relating us to our God in and through other believers.

By no means do we imply that we do not need to go to God alone in moments and hours of personal, quiet prayer, but if it is truly the God of Jesus whom we seek, our solitary prayer will constantly involve, touch on, impact all our other relationships and our entire world.

Christianity has been plagued by an early and continued heresy of Pelagianism, the belief that we can "earn" grace, merit gifts, win God's love. We have frequently fostered a kind of Avis spirituality that tries harder to compensate for being second best. In the light of this heretical tendency, much spirituality has sounded like the struggle to lift ourselves by our own bootstraps as we constantly fall on our behinds. There is a necessarily passive element initial to Catholic spirituality: "God has first loved us" (1 Jn. 4:11). It is because we are loved that we respond. Prayer (or life) is not a way to earn, merit, or achieve by our own concentration the love and blessing of God. We dispose ourselves to receive. We await a divine initiative. We remember what we have already been given.

Spirituality consists not in becoming more and more responsible in the fulfillment of a duty, but in becoming more and more faithful in a love relationship.

If we could capture what we mean by spirituality, and, as will become clearer, by spiritual direction, it would perhaps come in the form of an image. Becoming holy, spiritual, is not nearly so much a question of running up a steep hill, carrying heavy weights and puffing deeply, as it is a letting go of the weights, letting go of the climb, and falling backward in trust, believing that we will be caught up in loving protective arms. It is not trying harder, but letting go.

There is much wisdom in the old joke about the man who falls off a cliff and is on his way down a two-hundred-foot drop. At about one hundred feet he grasps a single, unsturdy branch. As he hangs there he cries for help. A voice comes over the side of the hill, saying, "Yes, my son." The man cries up, "Who are you?" The voice answers, "I am God." The man says "Help me." The voice says, "Certainly." The man questions: "What do I have to do?" The voice says, "Let go of the branch." The man looks down, looks up, and pleads: "Is there anyone else up there?"

In *The Empire Strikes Back* we cannot help but recall Luke Skywalker in mortal danger before Lord Vader, the shadow of evil, having to let go of the only thing he had to hang onto, trusting that the Force would indeed be with him.

Spiritual direction, in a way, is to become part of the catching process, part of the process that frees another to "let go." As we turn to a more specific effort to define spiritual direction, we know that the term *spiritual* is inadequate if we mean "spiritist," separate, disembodied. We focus more accurately if by *spiritual* we mean the human person under the influence, guidance, power, wisdom, love of the Holy Spirit.

NOTES

1. Walter M. Abbott, S.J., ed., *The Documents of Vatican II* (New York: Guild Press, 1966), pp. 199–200.
2. Matthew Fox, *On Becoming a Musical Mystical Bear* (New York: Paulist Press, 1976). See the Preface, especially pp. xviii-xx.
3. Thomas Merton, *Contemplation in a World of Action* (New York: Doubleday & Co. 1971), pp. 155–156.
4. Walter M. Abbott, S.J., ed., *The Documents of Vatican II,* p. 25 n. 9.

3 DEFINING SPIRITUAL DIRECTION

Out of his infinite glory may God give you the power through his spirit for your hidden self to grow strong, so that Christ may live in your heart through faith (Eph. 3:16–17).

Spiritual direction: an interpersonal relationship in which one person assists others to reflect on their own experience in the light of who they are called to become in fidelity to the Gospel.

This definition, this opening out of another's inner spiritual freedom, another's inmost truth, what Paul calls one's "hidden self" that grows strong, provides the subject for this chapter.

Admittedly, the term "spiritual direction" is woefully inadequate, for what we speak of is neither "spiritual" nor "direction." Our concern is not simply with the spiritual but with the whole person: body, mind, and spirit. We are concerned not simply with the life of prayer but with the entire faith-life. Our concern encompasses the whole human being, embracing every deed and attitude, every thought and feeling, every job and relationship constituting the unique person before us.

We do not speak of the spiritual part of a person if that implies what is disengaged from mind and body, what is "otherworldly." Our concern is not solely, though it may at times be primarily, with what goes on in the privacy of our prayer, but with the whole of life as it leads from or leads to that prayer. All of life is or can be theophany, and our concern is with all the instruments and melodies, all the notes and movements of the song. So "spiritual direction" is not simply "spiritual."

Neither is it "direction" in the sense that the director is the one who tells the other what to do or how to do it. To the extent that there is a director in one's life of faith, that director is always and everywhere the Holy Spirit. Our much more modest role is as helper, enabler, as others discover or establish direction in their own lives. Our relationship is not that of a guru to the uninitiated, or of a parent to a child, or of a teacher to a student, but a relationship that does whatever it can to facilitate God's own direction of us in our lives. We are more accurately described as beggars going out together, helping each other search for food.

Perhaps the director does have more experience, certainly a bit more objectivity, and sometimes more knowledge, but, still, both parties of the relationship travel together a road always respected as mysterious to each. We have perhaps been scarred or have seen others scarred by the director who *knew* what was best for us or for another, who *knew* God's will, who had the secret road map for another's journey. Our understanding of spiritual direction is more messy, less clear, more human, more searching, more conscious of the earthenware nature of our ability to lead another.

Sheldon Kopp's description of the psychotherapeutic relationship in *If You Meet the Buddha on the Road, Kill Him!* seems apropos:

> My only goals as I begin work are to take care of myself and have fun. The patient must provide the motive power of our interaction. It is as if I stand in the doorway of my office, waiting. The patient enters and makes a lunge at me, a desperate attempt to pull me into the fantasy of taking care of him. I step aside. The patient falls to the floor, disappointed and bewildered. Now he has a chance to get up and try something new.

Kopp goes on to ask what value the counselor or director then has, and he answers his own question:

> He provides another struggling human being to be encountered by the then self-centered patient, who can see no other problems than his own. He can in-

> terpret, advise, provide the emotional acceptance and support that nourishes personal growth, and above all he can listen.[1]

So spiritual direction is not in any narrow sense only about spiritual things, nor is it in any paternal or maternal sense directing. Further, it is similar to, but distinct from, both psychological counseling and the sacrament of reconciliation. What happens in spiritual direction depends on the relationship between two individuals. There is no specific undeviating blueprint. It touches deeply at the heart of what human relationships are and what it means to help another.

A spiritual director is often, but never exclusively, a *counselor.* In order to descriptively separate the roles of director and counselor, we can spell out two key processes in spiritual direction: one generally common to either counselor or spiritual director, one much more proper to the spiritual director. The first process concerns the objectification and articulation of experience; the second deals with the interpretation of those experiences through the eyes of faith, an interpretation sometimes called discernment.

OBJECTIFICATION AND ARTICULATION

Nothing a director does is more important than to be a listening ear for another. We would even seriously suggest that if you do not have a spiritual director, you would do well to draw an ear on the wall and talk to it. The director may be an improvement on the wall, but, initially at least, we serve the same purpose. In Taylor Caldwell's *The Listener,* the importance of one who listens quietly, receptively, nonjudgmentally is clearly brought out as numerous healings take place without a single word spoken by the mysterious "man who listens" on the other side of a veil.

The chief reason that anyone talks to another about the personal dimensions of life (whether it be a friend over coffee, a trusted teacher in school, or a well-paid psychologist in a formal office) flows from the deep human need to objectify—

to get whatever is inside outside. We need to speak to another in order to put our deepest feelings, fears, hopes, and dreams out in front of ourselves where we can look at them. The very process of articulation can itself be a healing experience. Directors and counselors begin with the awareness that their initial role is simply to be there as a sounding board, a friend. What we say is not nearly as important as what we hear and the opportunity we provide for others to speak out about who they are and what they are experiencing.

For either counselor or director no fixed boundary delineates what is proper for discussion. We concern ourselves not solely with prayer any more than the good counselor's concern is only with aberrant behavior. The subject matter is the whole person, and all of life is raw material for the dialogue. Whatever is significant to another person is significant to the listener. In the past, spiritual direction too often limited itself to the hour of prayer, the movement of specifically religious reflection in a person's life. But prayer cannot be separated from all of life. Nor are feelings, moods, impressions, and fantasies irrelevant. We need to express and own all our feelings, emotions, and movements of life. The listening role also enables another to objectify these.

Body language, the unspoken word, and the tone of voice also help to constitute the data of objectification, and the skilled listener "hears" these. Sometimes the use of a journal, a song, a poem, or a picture may help to externalize the deepest feelings and become apt subject matter for direction. We can invite people to draw how they feel about God, about their other relationships, about themselves, sketching the picture even in rough stick figures. We do whatever we can to creatively help another see. At this stage of the relationship the listener speaks little, asks supportive questions, clarifies what is obscure, and allows silence so that what has been spoken may sink in.

As the listening process (the objectification stage) continues, the counselor or director may assume a more active role and engage in some response, still helping the objective person to emerge.

The director or counselor enables others to become more

accountable to themselves. Even within the listening stance, we may at times *affirm, confront* or *teach.* We listen in order to affirm whatever is alive and growing in the other. Most people have very poor self-images and find their stories discouraging and depressing or, worse, boring. The sensitive listener hears the bright spots and underlines them. If people do not know their gifts, how important it is to have another point them out!

An honest listener also knows when to confront. Active, compassionate listening helps to unmask illusions, indicate inconsistencies, and recall spoken aspirations and admitted performance. There is a deep service rendered by a listener who lets some air out of an overinflated balloon before the whole thing bursts.

The spiritual director or counselor, still within this objectification role, may also at times be a type of teacher called upon to clarify theological or other human realities. Part of the objectification entails getting the facts correct, and, sometimes at least, simple instruction is called for.

INTERPRETING THE EXPERIENCE

In the initial stages then, direction and counseling are quite similar. Both aim at helping people to externalize whatever is in them and to look at it more clearly. Just as various schools of counseling will do quite different things with the material once it has emerged, so the task of spiritual direction deals with this revealed person in a unique fashion. The second role of a director seems to us to differ significantly from the role of psychiatric counselor or psychologist. The spiritual director specifically desires to help people to see their experience in the light of faith, to see the journey as a *faith* journey, to envision and trust God's guiding hand in the process. Both director and directee desire to take the raw material of this objectification and discern where God is calling, speaking, challenging, leading.

The definition of spiritual direction with which we began this chapter spoke of "fidelity to the Gospel." This fidelity is an agreed upon goal of the spiritual direction relationship. By Gospel we do not mean, primarily, the written word, but rather him about whom the word is written and who is, in fact, the Word. We luxuriate in a spiritual direction relationship, in a mutual effort to comprehend, to love, and to follow Jesus, the Christ. This agreed upon aim affects the whole relationship and gives us as directors permission to help others to organize their lives around the life of Jesus.

So, there resides in the midst of any crisis (divorce of parents, death of loved ones, problems in a relationship, vocational decision, etc.) a call to grow, to stretch, to risk. Put in Christian terms, each challenge offers an invitation to incarnate in a new way the death-resurrection mystery at the heart of our lives.

Outside of crisis times, over the long haul of life, the director enables a person to see rhythms and patterns, to discern what past decisions led to deeper union with the Lord or to more freedom with others. In the midst of a deepening interpersonal relationship the director becomes progressively more able to indicate the moods and moves that make the directee feel and be more authentic.

The ideal director does not judge, does not react *to* the person, but *for* the person and loves that person no matter what.

This role of interpreting experience fits into the archetype of Judaeo-Christian truth, the exodus event. Everyone, like our Jewish forebears, is called gradually from slavery to freedom, from some kind of Egypt to a new promised land. We all grow weary on the journey; all of us have moments of great closeness with the God who guides us by a pillar of light or feeds us with mysterious manna. We all have passed dry-shod through some threatening seas. We are all tempted to forget the guidance on the journey and feel abandoned, alone, confused and wandering. The Jews struggled to remember who they were and where they came from. They retold the story over and over to each other so that they would never forget God's goodness to them. They remembered, celebrated and built their corporate future on God's mighty deeds in their behalf. Each believing individual mirrors this archetype. We need a community, even of one, to help us interpret our story, to see it too as exodus, to view our private history as sacred history, to be conscious of the covenant God has made and kept with us.

The central thing that distinguishes the director from the counselor is, then, the agreed upon project of "fidelity to the Gospel." Consequently, they differ significantly in the way that conclusions are reached. It would be too generalized to insist upon, but, as a pattern, most counseling works through a process of interaction between two people, counselor and counselee. In spiritual direction the director is constantly aware that the real director is the Holy Spirit, and that the interpretation of the experiences may more properly and ultimately come from God out of prayer, rather than simply in dialogue between the two parties.

Concretely, as a counselor, we may continue to talk with a person until clarity comes, some pattern emerges, some action presents itself or, at least, some line of continued personal reflection emerges. We may do this over several sessions, but ultimately we are the primary other voice helping others reach conclusions for themselves. As a spiritual director we will more precipitously stop our conversation and invite another to pray, suggest a pertinent Scripture passage, or invite a period of prayerful reflection on whatever we are discussing, believing with that person that the Lord will help sort out the questions, provide the links, and indicate the next direction. We would, in other words, turn the person to the source of faith and not rely only on our conversation or the other's isolated reflection for whatever streams of interpretation will arise.

Scripture does not provide magic answers. We do not believe so much that "Jesus is the answer" as that "Jesus is the one who helps us live with the questions." Prayer is not an escape from grappling with those questions. But the relationship in spiritual direction begins and ends with the belief that God is calling each of us to become a unique person in light of the Gospel, that is, in relationship to Jesus Christ.

The one we work with discovers what that call is—not primarily in relationship with us, but rather with Jesus.

Again, it is too universal to be totally valid, but in general counselors need to step aside from their own presumptions, values, systems, and let the other be, with guidance toward that person's own chosen goals, goals that may differ significantly from the goals or visions of the counselor. This is partially true of the spiritual direction relationship, but with one enormous exception: spiritual direction involves a previously agreed upon, generally shared vision and desired goal (however that may be described: doing God's will, building the kingdom of the Father, forming one's life according to the Gospel). So where we, as director, would not normally judge or correct others in their vision, we do have, in the deepest sense, the mandate to challenge them to the Gospel who is Jesus. As a director we are not just enabling people to reflect on and and integrate life, as any good counselor would do, but to do so in the light of "who they are called to become in fidelity to the Gospel." This meeting with Jesus in faith is the decided and distinct difference between counseling and spiritual direction.

A second and related difference is that the end of the two relationships seems different, at least in nuance. Spiritual direction does not aim only to enable others to feel good about themselves, their God, and their world. Within a Christian context the mission of the Church is always central. The aim of spiritual direction is *charity* and *mission.* We are a people engaged in a project of fashioning the world in Jesus. We have had enough people burn out in their efforts to light the world on fire. We see ourselves very deliberately as part of the bellows that fans the fire and helps it to stay alive and burning. But the fire is to warm the world, the kingdom, not just the one we are directing. Though we may deal with the personal, private parts of one's life, we hope to be conscious, and assist another to be conscious, of the call outward as well as inward. The director is a filter helping others to experience God's love, supporting, trusting, and encouraging their knowledge so that "as God has first loved us, we can also love one another" (1 Jn. 4:11). The spiritual director sees success in terms of the engagement in apostolic mission and not merely of the mental health of the directee.

These remarks on the definition of spiritual direction, and its two central processes might best be brought to a close by a glance at a simple but clarifying schema.

(On part of director)	(On part of the directee) Known	Unknown
Known	arena of free activity	blind side
Unknown	secret self	subconscious unconscious

1. *Arena of free activity:* known to both director and directee. This is what is available to the individual and to others for themselves and for service. This comfort zone needs constantly to expand, increased by a greater comfort with the known but secret self, and by the unknown blind side and secret self. As directors, we hope to help others to become more and more who they uniquely are, more comfortable with that unique person, and more able to freely give that person to others, to all.

2. *The secret self:* generally known to the individual but not always trusted or loved. One of the most common parts of the secret self is one's relationship to God, the whole gamut of religious experience. We do not easily share this with others, and gradually we do not trust the experiences we have and are unable to build our lives on them.

There are other parts of our secret self that often do not show even to God because we are ashamed (e.g., our sexuality, our fears, our anger).

Part of the director's role is to enable others to let this secret self become more acceptable both to themselves and to others. Both the good and the bad can become available to God. These hidden aspects of the self can be made available to others when it is appropriate. We are trying to know God's love in all of our being. Who we are must be shown to be loved.

3. *The blind side:* that part of a person that others can see easily or with care, but of which the individual is personally ignorant. Often this blind side entails our very best traits and most obvious virtues. Someone needs to help us see our goodness, which we seem to deny. And even the less good parts of ourselves (perhaps a trait that hurts others by cutting them or a way of speaking that is often misunderstood, etc.) needs to be known so that it can be redeemed. The director is often primarily able to help others to see the previously unacknowledged good and bad.

4. *The subconscious or unconscious:* involves that whole complex beneath the surface of a person's personality that remains unknown to a director and directee alike, unless it is probed. The probing needs to be done with care and with some expertise. Though this is a spiritually valuable arena where God often speaks to us in dreams and fantasies, or where our roots are born in family and cultural archetypes, one needs a competent guide when entering these depths. Not all directors will be comfortable here, nor may they be helpful. However, it is a domain proper for one who cares to learn.

We began this chapter with the simple prayer about our hidden selves becoming strong as Christ lives in our hearts. What that prayer means may now be a bit clearer in this unique and precious relationship of spiritual direction. In the succeeding chapters we will discuss further the overlap between counseling and directing as we look at the presuppositions of anyone in a helping relationship. We will then deepen our dealing with the spiritual by several chapters focusing specifically on prayer.

NOTES

1. Sheldon Kopp, *If You Meet the Buddha on the Road, Kill Him!* (New York: Bantam Books, 1979), pp. 4–5.
2. See the introduction by John H. Wright, S.J. in "Two Discussions: (1) Spiritual Direction, (2) Leadership and Authority," in *Studies in the Spirituality of Jesuits,* IV (March 1972), pp. 41–51.

4 PRESUPPOSITIONS OF THE DIRECTOR

If our life in Christ means anything to you, if love can persuade at all, or the spirit that we have in common, or any tenderness and sympathy, then be united in your convictions, and united in your love, with a common purpose and a common mind. . . . In your minds you must be the same as Christ Jesus (Phil. 2:1–5).

A friend of ours used to use tarot cards when he began to direct a retreat. He read the cards as a way to begin to get to know the directee. As he improved at the "readings," he began to suspect things about the person he was talking to, things that did not show up in conversation until the fifth or twenty-fifth day. He quit using the cards because he did not want such suspicions to color his direction of people or to inhibit their freedom.

Some time ago one of us did an unlikely but revealing study of the *Playboy* Advisor over a period of six months. The intention was to discover the "morality" at work in Hefner's advice. An extremely coherent vision arose. Anything was all right if it did not hurt anyone *right now.* What was wrong and advised against was whatever caused pain to another in the immediate present. The future effects of actions were never an issue.

The point of each of these examples is to establish that those who enter into a helping relationship with another human being do so as specifically embodied spirits with their own attitudes, expectations, convictions, and presuppositions. The notions that we bring with us color the ways in which we relate with another. Tarot cards or the wisdom of *Playboy* is probably not our own bias, but biases we do have, and we need to name and own them.

Throughout this chapter we propose reflection on your biases and presuppositions. We will do this by reflecting on our own. We share with you our own theoretical framework regarding such topics as human motivation, affectivity, freedom, consciousness, and conscience, not so much in the hope that you will agree with us (though we hope you may) as that you take an honest look at what *you* believe. What do you think about the human person and the process of growth? In common parlance, "Where are you coming from?"[1]

HUMAN MOTIVATION

Why do people do what they do? Our way of answering this apparently simple question will greatly influence our approach to people. If we believe in tarot cards, we also believe that the future is predictable and predicted and that the strivings of an individual will not do much to change the outcome. If we are devotees of astrology and believe that the stars effectively determine human behavior, our respect for individual control will be severely limited. If we believe in God as a gigantic puppet master, controlling people's lives and causing the details of their existence, we will logically encourage people to *accept* their lives rather than direct them. If we believe people to be determined genetically, our healing work will be to learn medicine and try to effect help through pharmaceutical means.

We believe that at the most basic level people do what they do *because they want to.* This sounds so simple. As directors, the most significant thing we do is to assist others to know themselves and to know what *they* want at the deepest level of human desire, choice, freedom.

Recently one of us talked at length with a young man in the mental ward of a city hospital. He constantly questioned: "Why is God doing this to me?" If the question remains on that level, we and God are powerless to help him. To the extent that he can touch his own deepest hopes and fears, he can begin to let God love him out of the place in which he found himself. Physiological factors were present and many other factors inhibited his ability to cope, but there was a strong element of choice both in his being there and in his ability to get well. There certainly are exceptions to this, and deep psychiatric problems lie outside the boundaries of our competence, but we do begin with the presupposition that people, to a large extent, choose, and are therefore responsible for, what they want to do and be.[2]

It is as if each human person constitutes a committee constantly sitting to decide life's questions and the behavior desired in a given situation. This committee has many members within, each voicing a particular slant—our fears, feelings, dreams, and hopes, our history and relationships, our memory, our various sub-personalities, and our reason. Hopefully, the chairperson of that committee is reason, deeply influenced and guided by affectivity. Descriptively the task of a human person appears to become more and more integrated, whole, "together," within that on-going meeting. All the voices need to be heard and listened to. Ultimately, at their best, people make choices that chart the direction and, over time, develop the person. Since this ability and responsibility to choose is at the heart of human motivation, the spiritual director aids another to reach a harmonious decision from this complex and fascinating committee.

GOD'S WILL

Beneath the question of human motivation lies the reoccurring query: "How does one find God's will?" The religious person, almost by definition, desires to do what God wants. People seek direction precisely because they want to be directed by and toward God. It makes a great deal of difference, obviously, whether our framework places God's will outside ourselves, pre-determined, written on some eternal scroll, or whether that will is inside, coincidental with our deepest desires. We believe that we discover the will of God within ourselves, taking into account all members of our personal committee. When we most clearly know ourselves, we best know where and how God speaks to us.

A priest ordained five years, loving the ministry, but finding constant tension in the style of life that priesthood includes (celibate, all male community, living in the same place one works, twenty-four hours a day on call, etc.) searches to discover

God's will for him in his future. Can he stay as a priest and not die as a person? Should he let himself die? Is it possible for him to move elsewhere and still be faithful to God? The presuppositions both of himself and of his director greatly influence how the search is carried out. If God's will is external to him along with all that he has experienced, all he is feeling and hoping for the future, then this will is immutable and determined. His decision must be to remain where he is. If God's will is discovered deeply within himself as he reflects on the importance of choices he has made, his need to be faithful to relationships he has built up as a priest, his love of ministry, and his continued ability to feel and be alive and life-giving to others, he may be led to a new choice, with this new evidence, and a much clearer picture of what the deepest self in him really wants.

God's will is not found in our doing whatever we want, acting on whim. God does not baptize our silly frivolous choices (though he does still love us). We believe God's will is found in doing what we want at the very best and deepest level of who we understand ourselves to be. This is quite different. The director's role is to help us to be honest and to search until that deepest self is discovered. To do so, we as directors need to know what we believe about the locus of God's will.

AFFECTIVITY

In the above situation of the priest deciding his future, we hope that he does not make the decision solely on the basis of his feelings or affectivity. However, they certainly need to be taken into account. We directors must consider seriously our attitudes toward feelings. What importance do they have, and how much attention must be paid to them? They can be ignored, but feelings are never buried dead; they will surface somewhere else. Feelings can totally dominate and determine a person's life; destruction of one kind or another follows. Feelings demand to be noticed, and healthy people *know* what they feel, *accept* those feelings, and are able to *choose* how to act in the light of those feelings. A breakdown in any one of these three stages creates both spiritual and behavioral problems.

Many people do not *know* what they feel, deny their feelings, and avoid dealing with them at all. We can distance ourselves from our feelings. I am not sad at the death of my father; I am not aroused at the sight of that lovely woman; I never get angry; jealousy is not part of my makeup. In a thousand ways we deny what is being experienced deep within us. The person who does not feel sadness at death begins to experience no emotion at all. Often when we never experience sexual attraction, we masturbate alone or suffer inexplicable tension headaches. When we never get angry, we destroy relationship after relationship with snippy cutting remarks. Buried feelings surface somewhere else. We need to know and name them.

It is insufficient merely to recognize feelings. Often we know clearly what we feel, and we feel terrible about feeling that way. We cannot *accept* ourselves with this feeling. Good persons cannot hate their mother. A priest should not have sexual feelings during confession. A mother never gets mad at her children. If we experience these feelings we are bad.

But feelings are not good or bad; they are just true. We cannot control or destroy the presence of this or that feeling by a simple act of the will. There is no moral content to a feeling, and no moral goodness or badness in our feeling, no matter what we feel. It is all right to feel anything; feelings are not a matter of choice.

It often seems to us that one of the simplest and yet most significant things a director does is to help people recognize these truths and accept themselves. They then know that God accepts them, along with their strong emotions, especially of sexuality and anger. We pray: "Lead us not into temptation," not "Deliver us from ever being tempted at all." If we had no inclination at all to evil, there would be no virtue in refraining from it.

We recall a woman we worked with who had an aged and very cranky mother. This woman had spent several years struggling with her own self-image as a result of her mother's demands and pressures all through her adolescence. Now she had her mother living in a retirement apartment near her home. She called her two or three times a week, saw her every weekend, and regularly invited her for dinner with her family. She really resented her mother for past abuses toward her and her children, she resented having to pay so much attention to her now, and she continually confessed the sin of not liking her mother. But her behavior toward her mother was marvelous. She was acting in a most loving way; in fact, because she felt so negative, she was compensating by being as gentle and kind as she possibly could. She was acting heroically. Still she felt terrible because of her feelings. How important to help her look at how she was acting, not how she was feeling, in order to help her appreciate her own deep goodness!

This example leads to the third step. Once we recognize and accept our feelings, we can begin to *choose* how we want to act on them. We can act with or against our feelings. We do not need to be determined by them even as we allow them to influence our decision. If we are healthy, we will be able to choose freely, neither forced by, nor ignorant of, our affective response. I am hungry for that orange; it's O.K. to be hungry; I'll eat the orange. I am strongly attracted to Joe's wife; it is natural to be attracted to her for she is a lovely woman; but I choose to be a friend to both her and Joe and not to pursue that element of the relationship. I am very angry with my supervisor; it is very natural to be angry when I am the least paid person in the office; I will talk to her and indicate how I am feeling and try to understand why this is happening.

In developing our presuppositions about feelings, we are hopefully communicating their importance. Though not absolute, they are significant. A spirituality that is coldly rational dehumanizes. Prayer that does not heed feelings limits the ability of God to act forcefully in our lives. The passionate movements of prayer and the affective movements of life are extremely significant features of anyone's journey.[3]

HUMAN FREEDOM

It is obvious that these various areas of human behavior interweave and overlap. The discussion of choice in the light of feelings obviously leads to the question regarding our presuppositions about human freedom. We say that Jesus came to set people free, and that the truth will set us free. But there is often within us, the more tradition-bound we may be, a mistrust of freedom that can become license. We know that experiences of freedom badly used can create enormous problems for ourselves and for others. It is important to say at the outset that the freedom we mean is Christian freedom, the freedom to love and to serve. We need to ask ourselves as directors if it is more important to us that people do the "right" thing, or the free thing. Would we prefer to have directees act out of fear and be safe, or act on their present conviction and take the risk of making a mistake?

Imagine yourself directing a woman who prayerfully considers going back to work now that her children are grown, despite the protestations of her husband. You have helped her in prayer to look at the entire issue, to listen to the Lord, to talk with her husband, to consider alternatives, and to plot possible future effects. She finally decides in her best judgment to accept a specific job, even though you believe this is a serious mistake. Are you at peace? Can you trust the freedom of another, even when you are fairly certain that the exercise of that freedom will create new and severe problems? This is a crunch question for anyone involved in the life of another. Within a Church that has, for many years, maximized the law and minimized personal responsibility, a spiritual director will constantly be dealing with one form or another of this question. As directors we presuppose that it is far more important that others make their own choice, not ours.

GROWTH, HUMAN MATURATION, CONSCIOUSNESS

Do we view ourselves as the directors of a settlement or as frontier guides? Do we desire to help others adjust comfortably to what is or to explore all the marvelous possibilities of what might be? We should have a basic stance toward these questions and know what it is, for it will deeply affect our dealings with those coming to us, perhaps merely to cope, but more likely to grow.

We believe that human beings constantly have to give up what they have for whatever it is that they do not yet have. They do this on the word of someone who loves them. We believe that Jesus constantly stands before us inviting us to get out of the boat and walk on stormy waters, saying: "Give up what you have, and follow me."

We are constantly in the process of redefining ourselves, surrendering unessential parts and discovering new and deeper realities within. A child struggling to take its first faltering steps is not unlike a shy person trying to develop the courage to reach out and risk rejection. A promiscuous person, struggling under God's leading love, tries to be honest, authentic, and faithful in a relationship, but slips and falls. This kind of struggle is at the very heart of human growth.

It is as if we are all on a trapeze, swinging. Just as we become comfortable on one bar we have to let go, and wait, our feet firmly planted in mid-air, for the other bar to come into our grasp. We can only let go, wait, and recover, because someone on the ground is shouting encouragement to us: "You can do it." God is the source of that encouragement, but the director is often the means for that encouragement to be heard and heeded.

CONSCIENCE

The area of conscience formation and development needs a fuller treatment than we can provide here, for the entire area is still developing under the influence of people like Piaget and Kohlberg.[4] Spiritual directors do need, however, to have some framework from which to guide others toward a truly adult and Christian conscience. This conscience may not be the same as that of our bishop or our mother. It will be our own, and fragile.

The language of Thomas Harris in *I'm OK—You're OK*

may be a handy tool to use with younger people. We need to discover who and what our "adult" looks like, in opposition to the "parent" who fills us with shoulds and oughts, or the "child" who acts in obedience or rebellion to variously received injunctions. We spend a good deal of the first half of life establishing, recognizing and accepting this unique adult person.

In Jungian terms, as people pass through this process and become "individuated" or psychologically whole, they pass through a series of births. Two of the most crucial for a director occur (1) as people become adults, liberating themselves from parental authority and fusion with father and mother, and (2) as people emerge amid the conflicts of middle age and discover their true self. The first passage often needs the gentle hand of a director as we assume personal values, make personal choices, and accept the responsibility for our life. It is a time of insecurity, of rebellion, of disorientation. A gentle hand is needed lest the director become a substitute parent.

Strangely, the next stage invites a person to give up the control won with such difficulty and to surrender that control to God and to the movement of the Lord within the inmost recesses of the human spirit. As William Johnston writes:

> As life enters its middle period this deeper personality awakens, begins to assert itself, and to rise to the surface of consciousness. It is now the conflict begins; Is number two friend or foe? This I do not know. I only know that number one is now captain of the ship and does not wish to lose control or be dislodged. And yet certainly, if vaguely, I realize that number one must die if number two is to be born. This can be an agonizing feeling and it may precipitate a great crisis.[5]

Small wonder if many or most people, shrinking from the sacrifice involved, never allow their true personality to be born, never become their true self.

At this stage of surrender and discovery of new life, the spiritual director is particularly important as friend, as support, as sharer in hope. This stage is so significant that we will treat it separately in Chapter 6, but here our point is simply to note the need for the director to be aware of the attitudes brought to such periods of darkness and growth, those key times of human development in a person's life, especially the life of faith.

LOVE

The final presupposition should ideally be the first, but also is the last, the middle, the all. We believe that our most basic stance as directors is the central significance of love. What is the most basic human value? Christian conviction? Perhaps it seems so obvious as to not need mentioning, but, for that very reason, it must be raised. When we direct others, how do we evaluate the success of these relationships? Is our primary concern whether or not they are truly growing in love? Are we helping them to become more able to care about others than themselves, to be more willing in large and small ways to lay down their lives for their friends, to let their grain of wheat fall into the ground and die? By this will people know that we are followers of Jesus, by our growth in love, and not by any other sign.

We do not choose to live the Beatitudes because they are reasonable. We do not by hard work and good direction become a Gospel person, a follower of Jesus, one who says in word and deed: "I live now, not with my own life, but with the life of Christ who lives in me" (Gal. 2:20). We are converted into it, changed by God's transforming love, renewed by the touch of that creative hand.[6] And so the director hopes to facilitate and encourage (but never control) this meeting of the person with the person of God. And we judge the effectiveness of our relationship by the depth to which this relationship has called the other to life, to love.

We do not judge effectiveness by what mystical experiences the directees may have had, by the amount of peace they enjoy, by the number of books they publish, or by how long they have endured a difficult marriage. First and central in our framework as Gospel companions to other human beings is the belief that we with others are part of a process of gradually putting on Christ and becoming ever more fully incarnations of the Father's love for his people.

We cannot but feel inadequate to this task, knowing as we must our own struggles to be more transformed, more loving. And for this reason our final presupposition is the simple observation that it takes more faith to direct another than to be directed, for we directors cannot but experience the great temptation to doubt that God can work through us. We are aided by experience, by our own life of prayer, and by the gradual recognition that God does indeed touch people in and through us; so we continue to say to another, "Coward, take my coward's hand."

NOTES

1. Here we are indebted to Leo Rock, S.J. whose unpublished class notes were presented to members of the Institute of Spirituality and Worship, Berkeley, Cal., Spring 1975.
2. For a further treatment of healing in this regard, refer to John Sanford's book *Healing and Wholeness* (New York: Paulist Press, 1977), Ch. 2, "Body, Soul and Wholeness," pp. 22–40.
3. William McNamara, O.C.D., *Mystical Passion: Spirituality for a Bored Society* (New York: Paulist Press, 1977). See particularly Ch. 1, "Mystical Passion," pp. 3–16.
4. For further treatment by Kohlberg see "Stage and Sequence: The Cognitive-Developmental Approach to Socialization," in David A. Goslin, ed., *Handbook of Socialization Theory and Research* (Chicago: Rand McNally & Co., 1969), pp. 347–48; "Continuities and Discontinuities in Childhood and Adult Moral Development Revisited," in Baltes and Schaie, eds., *Life-Span Developmental Psychology: Research and Theory* (New York: Holt, 1972); Kohlberg, "Moral Stages and Moralization," in Thomas Lickona, ed., *Moral Development and Behavior* (New York: Holt, 1976).
5. William Johnston, *The Inner Eye of Love,* p. 147.
6. This notion of not *choosing* to live the Beatitudes but *being called* into them is developed in John Topel, S.J., *The Way to Peace: Liberation Through the Bible* (New York: Orbis, 1979), Ch. 9, "The Christian Response(ability)," pp. 119–131.

5 PRESUPPOSITIONS ABOUT PRAYER

It happened some time later that God put Abraham to the test. "Abraham, Abraham," he called. "Here I am," he replied. "Take your only child Isaac, whom you love, and go to the land of Moriah. There you shall offer him as a burnt offering, on a mountain I shall point out to you."

When they arrived at the place God had pointed out to him, Abraham built an altar there, and arranged the wood. Then he bound his son Isaac and put him on the altar on top of the wood. Abraham stretched out his hand and seized the knife to kill his son.

But the angel of Yahweh called to him from heaven. "Abraham, Abraham," he said. "I am here," he replied. "Do not raise your hand against the boy," the angel said, "Do not kill him, for I know you fear God. You have not refused me your son, your only son."

The angel of Yahweh called Abraham a second time from heaven. "I swear by my own self—it is Yahweh who speaks—because you have done this, because you have not refused me your son, your only son, I will shower blessings on you. I will make your descendants as many as the stars of heaven and the grains of sand on the seashore. Your descendants shall gain possession of the gates of their enemies. All the nations of the earth shall bless themselves by your descendants as a reward for your obedience" (Gen. 22:1-2, 9-13, 15-18).

When we worked in Lesotho, a small black country in southern Africa, giving retreats and workshops and generally talking about prayer, we ran a small informal survey among many of the people with whom we worked. We asked everywhere and often the simple question, "Why do you pray?" We received a variety of answers: "To show God I am sincere in my religious beliefs," "To be faithful to my religious commitment," "Because it is a rule and I am supposed to," "I am afraid not to," "It makes me feel better, closer to God," "It helps me to get through the day," etc. As you read this chapter we invite you to live with the simple question: Why do *you* pray? What do you hope to gain from prayer? Why should others pray?

There are diverse books of relative merit about prayer. Every week we see another advertisement for a new book on this subject. It may seem superfluous to treat of prayer in brief and inadequate fashion here. Still, we cannot speak of directing people in their prayer lives without serious attention to the subject most closely, but not exclusively, at hand. We hope in this short space to offer a reflective description of our own presuppositions about prayer as it flows into and out of the whole of life. We indicated in the previous chapter how important it is that directors be aware of their theological and psychological framework regarding the human person. It is perhaps even more necessary that directors know what they believe (and do not believe) about prayer. Again, we offer our reflections, not entirely so that you will agree with us, but as a modeling process to lead you to awareness of your own framework as you enter into dialogue with another.

Matthew Fox uses a definition for prayer that seems both concrete and general enough to umbrella our reflections. He calls prayer "a radical response to life."[1] The final word can be understood as Life, as in life-force, God, or as life, with the lower case indicating the daily occurrences that make up our existence; perhaps the two are the same. Prayer is, at base, a growing interaction with our own life in and through the Life who is God, an interaction that is "response" because God initiates and sustains the process. We are invited to be receptive to his initiative and to respond to the movements that occur throughout life. Prayer is "radical" in the sense that (as will be dealt with in our final three chapters) it gets at the very roots of our life, uprooting us, creating the new person of the Gospel. This definition, "radical response to life," is our first presupposition.

LIFE

As a "radical response to *life*," prayer is not concerned with the mere saying of prayers. It involves opening up to the Lord in all that touches us. Our daily joys (celebration of birthdays, reunions, breathtaking scenes of nature, a play or concert, time spent with an old or new friend) and pain (distance from someone we love, physical illness, misunderstanding, depression, a boring breakfast or a sleepless night) and the day to day, ordinary and extraordinary events and moods of our lives provide the substance of prayer.

Biblical persons strongly believed that God encountered them through the prophets, nature, and the law, but especially in the day to day situations and events of life, both of the individual and the community. We seek a return to that faith-vision where no part of our existence excludes God. There is no dichotomy between praying and living, between the sacred and the profane. Life and the beings who live it are one.

In a recent brilliant little book. *The Bush Still Burns,* an episcopal priest who had spent years trying to pray an hour in the morning, to make an annual retreat, to do all the standard exercises his calling insisted upon, tells how he finally became a praying person, meeting God one morning as he was walking across the Boston Common, a walk he had taken thousands of times. He, like Moses, was standing on holy ground as he stood on the ground he always stood on and went about the tasks he had always performed.[2]

Prayer, then, is not a part of living, a thing that is on our schedule that we "do," but all of living. It is not just a part of our thoughts, emotions, and feelings, but all of them. As Henri Nouwen puts it in an excellent chapter in *Clowning in Rome:*

> To pray does not primarily mean to think about God in contrast to thinking about other things, or to spend

> time with God instead of spending time with other people. Rather it means to think and to live in the presence of God. As soon as we begin to divide our thoughts into thoughts about God and thoughts about people and events, we remove God from our daily life and put him in a pious niche where we can think pious thoughts and experience pious feelings.[3]

This partitioning of life splits prayer and living, God and us. When we consider "distractions" those things that are not pious or religious, we are not letting God be for us in all of our lives. We could *almost* say there is no such thing as a "distraction" in prayer, but merely the experience of God providing the agenda. If we plan to pray over a Gospel story that tells of Jesus in the temple and begin to think of a relationship in our lives where we are not at peace (or are very much at peace and in love) this hardly constitutes a distraction from God, but the very stuff of that relationship with a God who is incarnate in our lives. We pick an obvious example, but it is just as obvious that there need be no part of our lives with which God is not concerned, perhaps more concerned than we.

This need not imply that we do not take quiet time apart from activity to pray, to be alone with God, but only that this exercise is not divorced from the rest of life. It is as if a little girl playing in the back yard knows her mother is present all the time. She goes about building sand castles, swinging, jumping rope, and playing with friends. Every once in a while she runs to her mother to express delight, to be comforted, to be noticed or nourished, to say "Look, mommy, at what I have made, or done, or been." But between these special times she knows her mother is there caring, watching, loving. We play constantly before the face of God, and everything in our life is a part of God's concern for us. Sometimes we make specific contact, or place ourselves immediately before that loving presence, but that is only to rediscover the truth of a presence that pervades everything.

And so all the activities of life—writing letters, teaching, visiting friends, nursing, cooking, typing, working in an office, talking on the phone, making love, encouraging, correcting, challenging others—all can be seen as prayer because we presuppose that prayer is essentially to be in a relationship with a living God who loves us, who, in fact, is obsessed with us. Prayer is life.

RESPONSE

Prayer is also life in *response* within a relationship. Probably the closest analogy we have for prayer is the intimate deep relationship between two persons who love each other profoundly: husband/wife, brother/sister, two very close friends. We think of our best relationship with another human being and begin to understand prayer. One of the best things about an intimate relationship is the ability to be our truest selves because we are loved and accepted as we are, and we know and trust this. We can say anything we want, share our greatest fears and failings, and rejoice in our greatest triumphs, confident that we will not be rejected. The loved one will be honest but gentle with us. Because we are loved we can trust, for "love casts out fear" (1 Jn. 4:18). We are not afraid to share the deepest core of our being or even our fumbling to understand that being.

Such trust develops out of time spent with the Lord on a regular basis in spite of how we feel, *believing,* in spite of dryness, or headache, or emptiness, or restlessness, that the Lord is working in us. Prayer has much to do, then, with believing that the Lord loves us as we are, rather than as how or who we would like to be. So if we are angry, we bring the anger to our God to be sorted out. We may even be angry toward that God. If we are lonely or depressed, we can be lonely before the Lord. The point is to be honest with God. If we cannot be honest with the Lord, we cannot be honest with others, or can be so only with difficulty. Each of us has a unique relationship with the Lord, so each of us relates to him in a way that no one else will, and to relate otherwise is to waste time, to be inauthentic, and to play games.

Two corollaries follow from this realization that prayer is a relationship. First, this way of looking at prayer heightens the importance of letting God love us. We are not trying to prove anything to God, or win points for fidelity, or show our good will to the people who make up our various communities. What we try to do in prayer is to experience deeply and consistently the undeserved, relentless love of God for us, despite everything.

Second, there is no sense comparing our prayer with anyone else's prayer, no matter what a temptation that may be. There is value in listening to others talk about their prayer, because we may gain new insights into God's activity, may vicariously experience his love as another experiences it, may deepen our own faith, may get ideas to try on our own. But we will pray as no one else prays. Sisters who live together, husbands and wives, and friends often compare their prayer, subtly, with each other, and often feel as though the other's is better than one's own—by some unknown standard. Such comparisons are futile. We want to relish the uniqueness of our own interpersonal relationship with our God.

To honestly attempt to be aware of the presence of this mysterious attractive Other in ourselves each day is to enter into a relationship that gradually makes us conscious of how much we cannot live without him. God becomes the center of our life. We are like a young woman who works closely with someone, enjoying his company, hardly noticing the time spent together, until one day he is gone, and she suddenly realizes that she cannot live joyfully without his presence. She longs to give herself to him completely and totally. When we do not pray, on the other hand, we belong too completely to ourselves. We remain our own territory, responsible for ourselves, struggling to reach the goal by our own efforts. When we pray, we know our need for another.

Prayer, then, is actually a process of falling in love, letting the Lord gradually draw us to himself. As we become more and more aware of his tenderness, his graciousness, we open our entire being to that love and wait on him. The paradox is that the more we surrender, give up independence as it were, the more we, like Abraham, find true freedom and blessing. Prayer, then, necessarily involves a growth in freedom—not the freedom to be whoever we want, but the ability to freely become who God is calling us to be; not the freedom to do whatever we want, but the freedom to love others as we have been loved, in ever widening circles.

Only love can change people; when we experience that profound sense of being totally and unconditionally loved for who we are (not as we would like to be) we are set free in a way that nothing, no one else can. We begin to receive our real identity or personhood.

RADICAL

As we assume our personhood, begin to be who we are called to be, or to grow into mature adult Christianity, we realize the truth of the presupposition that prayer is also radically a *risk* and a *challenge.* Any love relationship challenges us, calls us to risk, to go beyond ourselves. The entire Old Testament is the story of God calling the chosen people to growth, fidelity, transformation—from slavery to the old ways, and old gods, and from themselves.

In Abraham's initial encounter with God, he is asked to trust and to move. He is called not only out of his land but out of himself. God does not issue this call to test us but to help our real self emerge. And part of the challenge is that we are always left with the awful power or the freedom to say "yes" or "no." We are free to preserve our carefully controlled prayer and our limited life, or to evolve into an entirely new person.

The constant temptation in any love relationship is to control or possess the other, but this is precisely what the Lord never lets us do. Prayer will involve the constant tension of letting the Lord more and more possess us, while we become less grasping and more open-handed in that embrace.

Let us put this another way. Prayer can be hard, even difficult. We have heard that before. But the difficulty is not that of trying harder, pushing more. Prayer is difficult just as trusting is difficult. Prayer is a struggle—not just to keep away temptations or distractions, but to let Another take over, to let ourselves decrease so that he can increase.

GIFT

To pray then means to open ourselves to the Lord in a profound, loving relationship that affects all our lives. But this is precisely gift. Our final presupposition: prayer is gift. Our attempt to be present to the Lord in private prayer and throughout all of our day does not create the Lord's presence; it simply helps us become aware of it. This is our way of saying we long to be beloved sons or daughters of the Father. It is to be caught up in the life of Christ who prays in us.

We sometimes speak of the grace of God as if it were a thing. Grace is not a thing; grace is a person, Jesus Christ. The grace, the gift of God, is Jesus. We pray because we have received; we act because the action is already going on. Jesus lives in us, prays in us, and how intensely depends a great deal on how much we open ourselves to him. Prayer is not so much what we do but how much we allow the Lord to do, to act in and through us, to gift us.

Imagine sitting on a hillside in a strange country with a language other than your own. A voice that you cannot understand cries out, from a figure whom you cannot see. You look, but the brightness of the sun is too great; you listen, but the sounds are strange and unclear. The only thing you can do is wait and see if the voice comes toward you, and the words become more familiar. This is prayer; this is gift. It only demands our waiting presence.

This waiting can be captured in two other vivid images of prayer. We used to watch a windmill near a retreat house in Lesotho. Its huge arms which spread to the sky remained inert until the whisper of a breeze moved it gently, or more forceful winds spun it rapidly. The windmill could only wait.

A bird soars in the sky coasting on a recent gust, waiting

for another before its wings again propel it onward. The breath of the mystic is God's breath, not the heavy panting of our own meager efforts.

Because my prayer is essentially to be caught up into the prayer of Jesus who prays in me, it is also linked with the prayer of others, for the body does not consist of one member but of many (1 Cor. 12:12). True Christian prayer will lead us from personal prayer to communal prayer, not just as an optional thing but as an experienced necessity, consequent upon the same spirit working within us. God's gifts to us are not just ours, but the community's, not just for our benefit but for that of others. Growth of prayer in any one area will require and include growth in every other area. Good liturgical experiences lead us back to private prayer. Faithful private prayer leads us to celebrate liturgies with more depth and integrity. All growth in prayer is finally coming to know and to love God and his people.

These reflections on prayer everywhere imply that the subject matter of spiritual direction is the entire gamut of one's life. We become a filter helping others to know God's love in all their being, as they accept the gift of prayer given to them, let God love them, and respond ever more radically to life.

NOTES

1. Matthew Fox, *On Becoming a Musical, Mystical Bear,* p. 49.
2. John Smith, *The Bush Still Burns* (Kansas City: Sheed, Andrews & McMeel, 1978).
3. Henri Nouwen, *Clowning in Rome* (New York: Doubleday and Co., Inc., 1979), p. 70.

6 PROBLEMS IN PRAYER

> *To those who believed in him, Jesus said: "If you make my word your home, you will indeed be my disciples, and you will learn the truth, and the truth will make you free" (Jn. 8:31).*

Lucy and Charlie Brown are talking. Lucy is, as usual, complaining feverishly. Charlie Brown says: "Well, life has its ups and downs." Lucy replies: "Why can't it just have ups and ups?"

Prayer too moves in rhythms, ups and downs. Very often we begin a direction relationship because someone experiences a difficulty in prayer with a concomitant difficulty in life, either flowing from the prayer, or causing the difficulty in the first place.

Prayer is a relationship to truth: truth about ourselves, our God, our world. Prayer strips away myths, balances unreal expectations, and concretizes visions. It would be unreal to expect this process to be entirely smooth sailing. As in every relationship, honesty and truth come with a struggle. The spiritual director often becomes a guide through various degrees of darkness. Therefore we need to develop as best we can the ability and sensitivity to discern the causes of that darkness, and, perhaps sometimes, to recognize that there is no "cause," but simply the personal call of a loving God inviting a person to move to a new and different kind of prayer, a new level of relationship.

In this chapter we will reflect on some of the more obvious and, generally, more easily dealt with blockages to prayer. The following two chapters discuss at great length two areas that are more apparent than real blockages, but still require sensitive and astute direction.

Difficulties in prayer, periods of dryness and darkness,

come from a variety of sources. Our non-exhaustive list may help to point out some directions to discernment.

ROUTINE

A marvelous young sister spoke with one of us recently. It was April, and throughout the year, since September, she had been following the same demanding regimen in her life. She rose at 5:00 A.M., went running, came back, showered, got a cup of coffee and prayed, ate breakfast, went to school, was in her office till about 5:00 P.M., came home for a few minutes of quiet, then ate dinner, went to a meeting, or saw parents or faculty till 10:00, got to sleep about 10:30, then got up the next day and started in again. She indicated that she was finding prayer really hard work, very dry and sleep-ridden. With astute insight it was suggested that she could change her schedule a bit, getting up perhaps a half-hour later, and spending two shorter periods of prayer, one in the morning and one after she came home from school. She did that till the end of the school year and found much nourishment in those shortened periods of prayer.

This somewhat obvious example is typical of many instances in which a person who has prayed for many years has settled into a form which eventually becomes empty. A good director can help people to spot such routine and free them to try other places, other postures, other content—longer times, shorter times, whatever they need to restore a freshness into a relationship with God. Often the most helpful thing we can do is to expand the boundaries of a person's prayer. Some suggestions you could make: Put aside Scripture for a while and just remember personal gifts. Simply make a review of your day, the one just finished, or the one coming up. Take a favorite psalm or prayer and go over it slowly, rhythmically, with your breathing. Take a single word or phrase instead of an entire passage and just sit quietly with it. Listen to a record, either classical music or some liturgical favorite. Try the Jesus prayer. Try writing out a prayer, saying whatever you want to God, or Jesus, or let God write you a letter. Do whatever you can think of to loosen up your prayer. Walk outside, lie on the floor, go to a different room. Sing, dance, be creative in your expression of love for the Lord. In other words, encourage people to do whatever they can think of to introduce vitality into these precious moments.

LOOKING BACK

The temptation to continue to return to what has worked in the past has very much the same effect as any other rut or routine. Often a catalyst to prayer has been a powerful retreat experience, a baptism in the Spirit within a charismatic environment, a marriage encounter which began to revolve around an extremely meaningful scriptural passage, or a cursillo that created a new and enlivened interest in the faith journey. Any of these experiences, and many others, can be the basis of a life of faith that becomes invaluable. We need to remember the ways God has touched us in the past so that we can trust into the future. But that often becomes a trap to return constantly to what worked in the past. Our God is a God of history, and so a God of the future, constantly calling us into a new relationship, not just a repetition of where he loved us before.

We have often had someone come to see us carrying the tattered notes of a thirty-day retreat made three or four years before. So much happened during those precious days. For several years a return to, and savoring of, those experiences nourishes and sustains us. But now they are not touching us in the same way. It is time to move on. The sensitive director often assists people to move from where they are to where they are to be.

The need to move to a new way of praying often accompanies a change in the pattern of one's life. Just as a family that moves to a new city, a new job, or a new house will usually discover that each member relates slightly differently to each other as a result, so will the same be true in our relationship with God. When anyone moves out of a school setting into a first job, prayer will most likely change also. A woman who finds her children in school and the pattern of her life changed will probably discover some change in her life of prayer. Both of us have worked in schools over the years and seen new teachers, religious and lay, begin about December to go into a deep spiritual slump. Among other parts of reality, their ways of finding God had changed and they had not yet discovered new ones to replace what they had given up. The awareness that a change in life-pattern often creates a need for a new pattern of prayer will allow a director to help a person to relax and discover where and when and how God is present now.

TRYING TOO HARD

One common problem in prayer arises simply from trying too hard. As James Finley writes in *Merton's Palace of Nowhere:*

> Merton once told me to quit trying so hard in prayer. He said: "How does an apple ripen? It just sits in the sun." A small green apple cannot ripen in one night by tightening all its muscles, squinting its eyes and tightening its jaw in order to find itself the next morning miraculously large, red, ripe, and juicy besides its small green counterparts. Like the birth of a baby or the opening of a rose, the birth of the true self takes place in God's time. We must wait for God, we must be awake; we must trust in his hidden action within us.[1]

The continued realization that prayer is gift, something God does in us, not something we do ourselves, frees us to relax, take the pressure off ourselves and wait, allowing God to come as he wills.

All the above blockages are relatively simple sources of difficulty in prayer. The following are a bit more subtle, requiring a more listening ear, a more gentle hand, and, sometimes, more direct guidance.

SELF-ABSORPTION

Prayer is, or ought to be, letting God love us. In prayer we pay attention primarily to God, not to ourselves. Our attention is with the Other. But faulty previous training, a personal sense of inadequacy, or a misunderstanding of the Christian life can lead us to focus primarily on ourselves, and thus to find prayer extremely difficult and painful. Prayer, strangely, becomes a mirror we hold up to show ourselves how awful we are. Every Scripture text, every religious thought, immediately becomes an indictment of our sinfulness. We read the Beatitudes and see not the glorious vision Jesus invites us to but, rather, all our myriad failures to realize that vision. We reflect on the story of the prodigal son and grovel with the son in the pigsty instead of being overwhelmed by the love of that Father who insists that we are not servants but beloved sons and daughters. We meditate on the passion of Jesus and focus on our own sins that crucified him instead of on One who laid down his life because of love of us.

Such prayer becomes too painful to continue and we simply cannot (and should not) enter into it anymore. We cannot endure a prayer that leaves us always liking ourselves less. Such experiences often lead to automatic, impersonal prayer—the recitation of the office, the obligatory attendance at Mass, the occasional recitation of other objective prayers, a growing flight from quiet, contemplative prayer because we feel so inferior afterward. We guide people to a clearer idea of God and of God's love and away from an intense and relentless preoccupation with themselves. How can we help another to meet a God who loves us more than he judges us, a God who looks at us and is more joyful that we are growing than disappointed that we have not yet arrived?

PATTERN OF SIN

The prophet Nathan functioned as a spiritual director for King David (2 Sam. 12:1-15). Once, when David was quietly wallowing in guilt, unhappy with himself and his kingdom, Nathan told him a story. It concerned a poor man who had only one lamb and a rich man who had many. The rich man had some friends coming over for a party, and instead of depleting his own flock, he stole and killed the poor man's only ewe. David was incensed and cried: "Show me the man, and I will punish him." Nathan replied, doubtless with a wry and careful smile: "You are the man." David was able to recognize and admit his sin—his stealing of Bathsheba and his killing of her husband. He repented, and his prayer, our psaltery, flourished again. Psalm 51 testifies to the effectiveness of Nathan's direction. He helped David see the connection between the whole of his life and his relationship with God.

Just as a whole marriage relationship becomes strained when the parties are not at peace with one element of that relationship, so we experience great difficulty in prayer when one part of our life is out of kilter, protected from God's gaze or even our own honest perception. We human beings are funny; we kid ourselves so well and rationalize so effectively. Often we know deep down precisely what is wrong, but we fool ourselves, ignore that awareness and try to pray. Prayer fails until another, some Nathan, points it out to us.

Our decision not to have anything to do with the next-door neighbor or not to forgive that woman who hurt me so much, a deep grudge against my boss or a young man down the hall—any breakdown in a human relationship that is accepted and clung to cannot but lead to the same breakdown in our relationship with God. Our lives and prayer coalesce, for God is part of all our relationships, and whatever we do to the least of his children we do to him.

This does not mean that we need to be perfect in order to pray. In fact the opposite is true, for only sinners (all of us) *need* to pray, to turn to God for love despite our failures. But we cannot be hardened in and denying of that sin. We block God out of our lives whenever we choose to block another out.

Any truly moral evil in our lives (dishonesty, theft, abuse of a drug or alcohol, mismanagement of our sexual lives) will ordinarily inhibit prayer if not admitted and brought into that prayer for healing. A person struggling with alcoholism may pray very well, but not if he denies the reality. People struggling to resolve a relationship that has become destructive for them or for another may pray very deeply and experience God's love for them in new ways. If the disorientation and disorder are denied, prayer will undoubtedly be blocked until this is brought to awareness and made available to God.

If prayer continues to be difficult for a person we direct, we often probe into the recesses of the other's life to see if some dimension is unspoken, guarded. And we may be asked to be a Nathan, pointing out by story, by gentle challenge, or by example from our own life the sin another fearfully holds onto.

GUILT

The director often helps unearth this blockage that flows from the presence of real moral evil in another's life. *Imagined* evil also creates a problem with prayer. It need not, but it does. Those who suffer from a false guilt experience the same absence of God, although they are more likely to be vividly, even morbidly aware why. Bad conscience inhibits prayer.

People most commonly feel *guilty* without necessarily *being* guilty in the areas of anger and sexuality. The example in a previous chapter about the woman who felt hostile toward her mother, while at the same time acting in an extremely loving way, exemplifies this blockage. She felt distant from God, alienated, even though she was acting in a most Christian way, because she did not give herself credit for how she behaved and focused only on the deep negativity in her feelings. Acceptance of feelings often easily heals this seeming separation from God.

Nocturnal emissions, feelings of passion, strong attraction, or even deep friendship can cause the same type of unnecessary but destructive guilt. We need to see that a life shared with an incarnate God will never be free from struggle and some inclination to evil, but can become one in which we refrain from sin because of God's love for us. Often the very source of guilt, misplaced, can be seen later as a wonderful sign of God's sustaining love, freeing one to enter more deeply into the love relationship of prayer.

A celibate woman entering into her mid-thirties is plagued by sexual fantasies and desires. Whenever she tries to pray, she is besieged by sexual desire and cannot come before God who could not possibly approve of this dimension of her personality, so new to her. Encouraged to bring those very fantasies to prayer, to let them occur as she sits before her God, to let God love her precisely with this new reality present, she experiences a new healing sense of God's love. This is but one way we might encourage people who suffer feelings of guilt, not rooted really in sin, to trust in God and to let go of the guilt, facing the truth of his love that will make them free.

APPENDIX TO BLOCKAGES IN PRAYER

The bibliography at the end of this book indicates many sources of information both for the director and the directee to creatively move from darkness to light. But it may be helpful here to indicate some simple aids to starting, or starting over, in prayer. They are more or less obvious, standard suggestions to help someone confidently enter again into a relationship that has never, or not recently, been alive.

We have a period of time to pray before us. What might we do with that time? From a thousand possibilities. we start, perhaps, with these.

Become quiet: Initially it is important to quiet myself down to pray. I enter into myself, get in touch, become aware of what I am doing. I breathe quietly, empty my mind of outside thoughts, perhaps speak a single word like "Jesus," or just become still, aware of my breath. I might use the Jesus prayer (Lord Jesus Christ, Son of God, be merciful to me, a sinner) in rhythm with my breathing. I might picture myself somewhere in the presence of my God. Whatever I do, I begin with some quieting time that will open me to accepting God's love.

Ask for what I want: Why do I come here before God today? What is on my mind or in my heart? What joy or sorrow lies in me needing to be released? What do I hope to receive during this time of prayer? It may help to ask God very specifically for what I want. "Lord, help me not just to know myself as sinner, but as loved and forgiven sinner," or "Lord, help me to know you better so that I can love you more and serve you more wholeheartedly," or "Help me, I'm falling," or "I want to thank you for the best day of my life," etc. I need to ask for what I want in order to be in touch with myself, for I am part of the prayer relationship.

Compose myself in place: Some find it helpful to let the imagination enter into the first stages of prayer. If I plan to use a Scripture passage, it may help to imagine the scene into which I am to immerse myself—the crib, the cross, the streets of Galilee, the hillside where Jesus speaks. Or I may in imagination place myself in a location where I will be at peace—a cabin in the woods I have always found so peaceful, a chapel I like, an ocean beach—even if I cannot be there physically now. I find a place within myself and locate myself there with the Lord.

I am a bodied person, and, therefore, I try to pray in touch with my senses, my feelings, and my body, and not merely with my mind. It is important to be with the Lord and not just think about him.

Turn to Scripture: Some do not know what to do when they take up the word of God and begin to pray. There is no wrong or right way to do it, and many simply discover their own way, which is ideal. But if someone wants to be assisted, a variety of approaches can be suggested. It even helps to walk through, and talk through, different ways with those I am directing. Pray with them to help them pray alone:

Read over a passage several times, not trying to analyze it but just letting it sink in slowly, or

Read it once slowly, letting it sink in bit by bit, even reading it out loud, or

Look it over, read it for the word or phrase that speaks to me, or a feeling that moves me; savor that word or feeling, or

Read the passage, close the book, and let God lead wherever I want, or God wants, or

Insert myself into the passage, the mystery (event in Christ's life), and simply live there with the Lord, just being part of the scene, one of the people, present, watching, attentive to the scene before me, or

Apply my senses to the scene, hearing the words, smelling the air, the animals, the flowers, feeling the mood, perhaps most importantly touching the Lord, or letting him touch me.

Let God lead: Most importantly, let God take the initiative. If I am moved to pray, pray; the passage need not be finished nor even begun. The above points are helps or aids, spring-boards to prayer. I may not need any of them. If I do not, I will simply pray, thank, and love without them.

Review: When I have finished my period of prayer it may help to evaluate what happened to me and what I did. Where was God present—or absent? What was good or difficult? Be ready to go back to those places of great consolation as long as they are helpful. And be courageous to return to those places that were challenging and difficult. It may be helpful to keep a journal, writing down these reflections for myself or my director.

Spiritual directors do whatever they can to help another when the "downs" occur. The above examples are some of the more easily diagnosed and dealt with. Much more difficult problems occur. We will deal with two rather common experiences in the succeeding chapters. First, a person may be moved by God from active to more passive prayer and experience a period of profound darkness. This is not something the director can help with very much except to be a support and a friend, a source of hope. Second, sometimes a person cannot pray about anything else until a major decision is resolved in life. The director can help a person use prayer to solve or settle a question and then be free to move on.

NOTE

1. James Finley, *Merton's Palace of Nowhere* (Notre Dame: Ave Maria Press, 1978), pp. 115-116

7 PRAYING THROUGH THE DESERT

Come to me, all you who are weary and find life burdensome, and I will refresh you. Take my yoke upon your shoulders, and learn from me, for I am gentle and humble of heart. Your souls will find rest, for my yoke is easy, and my burden light (Mt. 11:28-30).

My God, my God, why have you forsaken me (Ps. 22:1)?

Recently a woman one of us directs exemplified one form of a common phenomenon. She began the conversation indicating that she felt she really had not prayed for two years. Asked if she did try to put some time aside for the Lord, she admitted to spending an hour a day, but to feeling nothing seemed to happen. How did she know that nothing was going on? She had no consolation in prayer, no lightness, no sense of God's presence, no insights to carry her through the day, none of the satisfying experiences she had relied on for so many years.

The initial effort to aid this woman involved helping her to look at the rest of her life, to focus on the changes that were going on inside her, and to pay close attention to the rewarding aspects of her life, her work, her relationships. She began to see the Lord in the children she taught and to notice a mellowing dimension in all her interactions with others. Her "prayer" did not change rapidly, but she began to be delighted with all the amazing things that were happening in and around her that she had previously not noticed at all. Eventually even her aridity in prayer provided a satisfaction of its own.

Sometimes what appears to be a blockage in prayer is rather a gift of God. Through darkness, aridity, and emptiness we are called to a new form of prayer, a new stage of our relationship with the Lord. The director learns to look at other possible causes, but to be aware that difficulty in prayer often marks the beginning of real prayer, prayer in which the Christian begins to seek, and to find not the consolations of God, but rather the God of consolations—a God often found precisely in darkness, nothingness. In this state, no natural exercise we can dream up, no method or procedure, no effort on our part or aid from another, nothing we can do can bring us into felt, vital contact with the Lord.[1]

Often, therefore, what appears to be the absence of prayer marks the transition from one form of prayer to another, specifically from discursive meditation to contemplation (often called, in fact, dark contemplation).

St. John of the Cross indicates three signs within prayer to help us determine that it is precisely this transition to which we are being called.[2]

First, one experiences the impossibility of making discursive meditation, of receiving the same satisfaction from it as before. No thoughts, no words form. Nothing seems to happen. There is no satisfaction.

Second, one experiences a growing inability in prayer to fix the imagination, to focus on a particular subject. What is known or perceived is not logical, but intuitive.

Third, despite pain or difficulty in the above two experiences, one also possesses a deep, growing desire for solitude, a longing to just be with the Lord. Although nothing seems to be happening, the desire for something to happen is stronger than ever, the desire to pray, the desire to make contact with the God who seems so far away. This often is accompanied by a deep anxiety about displeasing God that needs to be gently dispensed with.

Besides John of the Cross' internal signs that this transition is occurring, we need to consider the entire life of the individual. We cannot judge our prayer, whether it be consoling or desolate, by how we feel when we pray, but rather by how we are loving when we live. Nor can we judge our prayer by what we say. The recognition that life is fruitful, Christian, loving (even with pain), coupled with the prayer experiences that John describes, enables us to help another to trust the call of God to a new and deeper relationship.

Thomas Merton indicates another way of looking at this experience.[3] The director perceives that another is truly going through an authentic "desert experience" and being called into this "prayer of faith," by the mere fact of an insistent seeking for him blindly, undauntedly, in spite of dryness, in spite of apparent hopelessness and the irrationality of the quest. This same person experiences, sometimes deeply and with great anguish, a sense of meaninglessness in life, a loss of perspective with regard to the meaning of everyday life. Finally, and paradoxically, the person persists in a desire to remain in that aridity, in spite of affliction and defeat. Again, perceptive insight into the rest of life helps the director and the directee to trust what is transpiring.

Personal experiences of directing others through these deserts yields for us the realization that one will, at the same time, both lean heavily on the director, and yet presume that the director has not heard, has not understood. Often people will feel that the experience must be due to some fault on their part, some missing piece to the puzzle of life. They want to find that piece. When the director assures them that they are going through a stage of prayer development, that they are all right, that they will not fall totally apart or lose their minds, they find it difficult to trust, to believe that they have been heard. It is a sensitive and delicate time, painful to the director as well as to the individual searching for God.

This remoteness of God needs to be read as a deepening of relationship and an invitation to the individual to focus consistently on who God is and what God is doing—to get the attention away from oneself, to avoid deep introspective analysis or personal strivings to do what is "right" in prayer. It is a call to abandonment of personal control over prayer, over the whole relationship with the Lord. It is an invitation to let God be God. It is as if God is having a difficult time making contact with us because of our remoteness, not God's. We need to be as totally present as possible and willing to wait.

We need to resist that temptation to "junk up" our prayer with business and activity, with reading more psalms, saying more rosaries, making more frequent stations, or reading even more passages of Scripture. It is an invitation just to wait.

In our experience, men find this especially difficult. Many of them (and some women too) simply stop praying at this time, or they become extremely formal in their prayer, preferring to maintain control. Often, at this point, a relationship with God, growth in spirituality, true holiness, or the ability to love and be loved stagnates. The Hound of Heaven is on our trail, but we are tempted to run with all our energies in the opposite direction. How difficult it is to stop and let ourselves be found!

In speaking of this transition in prayer, it may seem that we are talking only of the "professional" praying person—priest, or religious, or exceptional lay person. In fact this phenomenon seems common in the lives of many sincere people who find that, somewhere in the middle of their lives, the Mass they had always treasured no longer moves them, and that their private devotions, once so consoling, are dry and apparently empty. We are convinced that many so-called average parishioners experience this important transition in their relationship with God, and that it is important for the sensitive pastoral person to help them name what is going on in order to pass into the new life that lies on the other side of this new pain.

Again, how important it is to help a person focus on the whole pattern of life and not exclusively on what is going on in prayer. Often, as prayer seems so difficult, life becomes fuller and richer. In prayer the Lord seems particularly absent, but closer attention to the whole of life reveals God's presence more frequently in every place. We look for that presence only in prayer, but it is revealed in the ordinary experiences of our life and ministry—in a moment of particular compassion for another, in a time of relaxation near a mountain, a river or a sunset, or as we sit by a fire sipping scotch with a friend. God is seen in new friendships, in the return of lost friends, in a giftedness in dealing with the sufferings or joys of another.

If all of life is understood as prayer, as a relationship, we begin to become gradually aware of the touch of God throughout the day, prepared for by this painful time of empty waiting.

Sometimes our expectations in prayer are quite unreal; we look for a kind of "ecstasy on schedule." Jesus did not experience this, and neither will we. What is often a difficult, even boring time for us can be very pleasing to the Lord. We will not be spoon-fed as we grow in this relationship.

Several times in this chapter we have referred to the need to look at the whole of a person's life to see the validity of that person's prayer, to test whether, in fact, the experience of God's absence is truly a call to a new stage of prayer. In what follows we indicate some of the things that are likely to be happening in people's lives as they grow in relationship to God. We suggest, then, some *criteria for evaluating the authenticity of prayer.*

These criteria require two preliminary notes. First, although we use them here to test whether "prayer in the desert" is truly that, they can be used to test the validity of any prayer experience. Someone may be going through wildly exciting charismatic flights of mystical experience; we need to test whether such joyous experiences are from God. We judge the fruitfulness of prayer by how we live, not by how we feel in prayer.

Second, all these criteria are inter- or intra-personal. In a later chapter we will look at social criteria that are equally necessary.

Some of the following signs will be present—proportionately present, more and more present, never completely present.

TRUST

As prayerful people, open to God, we will grow in trust—trust of God, of ourselves, of others. Faith deeply assures us that as long as we say "yes," God will lead. This sense of being led grows and becomes more comfortable. We learn to "let go, and let God." This is both a prerequisite for prayer and a sign of its authenticity.

GENTLENESS

As prayerful people, we gradually become more mellow, more loving, more gentle, more compassionate with ourselves and with others. We become more at home with our own infidelity and weakness, but also more at home with God's love. A sense of freedom, of being "opened up," accompanies real prayer. We may be sinners, but we are called, loved, chosen and redeemed sinners.

Thus we become less depressed by our own failures and no longer feel a need to prove ourselves. The deep sense of being "gifted" flows from the absence of any fear of losing God's love, so unearned in the first place.

LOSS OF FEAR

As we pray, we become less concerned with "looking good," need less to hide our faults from others, and worry less about the impression others have of us. God is loving, and there is less fear as perfect love (doing its work) casts out fear (1 Jn. 4:18).

FOCUS ON GOD

As we grow in prayer there is less and less focus on ourselves and more and more on God. The sense that Jesus had of Sonship with the Father becomes our sense. We see ourselves as sons and daughters of God. At the very core of our being we find ourselves crying out, as Jesus did, "Abba, Father."

UNICITY

In all of this our prayer becomes more uniquely our own, and, consequently, more difficult to talk about. The richest retreats are often those in which the director hears very little and says next to nothing. We cannot talk about our prayer with clarity, except that it is all right. The director can only be there to support the unique love going on between the directee and God.

AUTHENTICITY

The desire for honesty and integrity grows as our relationship with God grows. This integrity is for others and toward others, a need for authenticity in all of life. Yet there are fewer highs and lows, and more congruence and consistency, both interiorly and exteriorly. We become, in other words, more simple, more "together."

FORGIVING

A certain non-judgmental quality grows in a praying person. We find it easier to forgive others and to ask their forgiveness. The relationship with a loving and forgiving God begins to concretize the "Forgive us as we forgive . . ." of the Lord's Prayer. Things that used to bother us pale into insignificance. Priorities become Christianized, and what is objectively important, the call to love, becomes personally important.

RECONCILIATION OF OPPOSITES

Within our whole lives, opposites begin to be reconciled. Action and contemplation are no longer two, but one. Truth is tempered by love, and love by truth. Waiting and action eventually seem less separate than they were, and one waits while acting, and acts while waiting. We find new strength in gentleness and a new gentleness in strength. The previous tension between caring for self and serving God, seeking self and seeking God, is no longer polarity, but fidelity to self united with fidelity to the forces that are forming us.

UNIVERSAL LOVE

The love in which we grow is not just for God, nor do we love others because we find God in them. We find ourselves no longer trying to love God in other people but loving God more precisely because of others. And this touches not just our special friends, but people we never before noticed or considered significant. The praying person experiences a growing ability to enter into the joys and sufferings of others and truly to care.

In all of the above, everything is seen and acted on in the light of our relationship with the Lord. The source of our actions is the freedom found in that relationship and not in external oughts or shoulds or the fidelity to various rules or laws. All things become a possible theophany, a sense that wonder is happening all about and within us, and we develop a greater capacity to risk in every area of life, dependent not on our own strength but on God's.

This brief summary statement of the kinds of things that happen in the life of one called into a deeper level of prayer, a deeper relationship with the Lord, can perhaps help the director to see God's hand working in the life of one who is temporarily unable to see it because God *feels* so absent. The interaction and harmony between life and prayer become tremendously important, and the good director resists every temptation to judge another's prayer life only by what is experienced or not experienced in those periods specifically devoted to prayer. Prayer becomes life, and life becomes prayer.

The wonders of God's revelation are shown to us in good times and in bad, in our sinfulness and our forgiveness, our sadness and our celebrations, in the desert and in the land that flows with milk and honey. Our God reveals himself gradually and in various ways, but always as a God whom we cannot know or fully possess, a God whom we cannot control or make perform consoling miracles upon demand, a God who can be trusted because he is loving Father to us.

NOTES

1. Thomas Merton, *New Seeds of Contemplation* (New York: New Directions, 1961), p. 39.
2. John of the Cross, *The Collected Works of St. John of the Cross,* translated by Kieran Kavanaugh, O.C.D. and Otilio Rodriguez, O.C.D. (Washington, D.C.: ICS Publications, 1973), Book 2, Ch. 13, pp. 140-141.

3. Thomas Merton, quoted in Raymond Bailey's *Thomas Merton on Mysticism* (New York: Image Books, 1975). Bailey cites a yet unpublished treatise on "The Inner Experience: Notes on Contemplation," p. 173.

8 PRAYERFUL DECISION MAKING

God, examine me and know my heart,
Probe me and know my thoughts;
Make sure I do not follow pernicious ways,
And guide me in a way that is everlasting
(Ps. 139:23–24).

"Should I stay on my job?" "I'm not peaceful in my priesthood." "Everytime I try to pray, I'm only conscious of how deeply unhappy I am in my marriage." "What school should I go to?" "If I leave the classroom, what will I do?" "I am so distracted by this or that uncertainty that I simply cannot pray."

Though the need for a major decision in a person's life may not be exactly a blockage to prayer, it demands direct attention before anything else can be the subject matter of that prayer. Nothing else will work until the decision is faced. A spiritual director often deals with someone needing to make a prayerful, God-centered decision in life. Such direction may occur within the context of an on-going relationship or form the basis of a new relationship at a crisis time.

A great deal of material has been written about discernment, or the time of election, in the *Spiritual Exercises of St. Ignatius.* This section will present a simple, clear outline of that method as it applies to individual decisions.[1] Other ways are good; this is one way.

First, the context. We face a major decision in life. Like most human beings, we have probably experienced "going around in circles," arguing with ourselves, weighing one side against the other with no visible movement forward in the process. We feel confused, unable to sort out thoughts or feelings, drawn to both sides of the dilemma, or, perhaps, equally repulsed by conflicting choices, one of which must be undertaken. We long for more calm, the ability to take a decisive stance. We also desire to make the best decision possible both for our own human, spiritual development and for the good of God's kingdom.

Second, the process occurs within the *Spiritual Exercises* almost two-thirds of the way through a thirty-day retreat, that is, only after a person has experienced a deep and personal call from Christ the King to follow him in suffering so that we may share with him in glory. This procedure depends, therefore, on a consistent life of prayer. It may be helpful simply as a secular exercise, but its power lies in a way of moving from "indifference" (a balanced openness to whatever God wants) to a particular life-stance toward which the God with whom we are in love moves us. In practice, we may need to step back from the immediate decision and begin by establishing a relationship with Jesus Christ that allows us to be open and free.

This method presupposes, then, (a) that we truly seek God's will in the midst of a life in which Christian values exist and endure, (b) that we honestly search for God's will (which is the same as our own deepest, best desire), (c) that we are truly "indifferent" in the best sense of that word—open to whatever seems the most life-giving, loving thing to do, and (d) that the choice is between *good* things, for there is little or no sense in praying about whether or not to rob a bank or commit a murder.

Granted these conditions, we hope to move toward a decision, break out of the circular internal arguing that paralyzes, and decide in a way that will not foster continual backward glances wondering if the decision made was correct. We also hope to make a decision that is our own and not that of a mother or father, a husband or wife, a provincial or spiritual director.

The first and easiest way to make a decision is to be knocked off a horse, as was Paul. If God dramatically enters our life and profoundly pushes in some direction, the need for confirming prayer is minimal, and then only to accept, not decide. But in less dramatic fashion, in the absence of such divine intervention, there is sometimes simply a profound sense of peace or rightness about a decision that does not demand a careful weighing of each side. When such a mood or feeling persists over a period of time, a director may help us to see and trust what has already been made clear, without engaging in a lengthy process. For example, a young man practicing law but who is not happy with the legal profession has the opportunity to go into teaching. He knows he can make more money as a lawyer, that it provides more security, and that he has spent a long time preparing for this profession, but he is simply not happy. Whenever he thinks of teaching he is profoundly happy, filled with peace. The thought has been with him, accompanied by this peace, for some time. He may find it difficult to decide because of many external pressures and the expectations others have of him, but deep down he already knows his choice and has a sense within his day-to-day life and prayer of what he wants to do. The director's role would only be to support him in the decision already made, down the path the Lord is already leading him.

But when there is neither a divine intervention, nor a deep and profound attraction to one side of a choice, when things are simply not clear at all, when arguments loom up both for and against either choice, we may enter into a more lengthy and structured period of prayer to aid that decision.

St. Ignatius suggests three simple exercises to prepare the soil, to test out initial, immediate prayerful reactions. We sometimes use these in the beginning of a process, and at times these simple exercises can be so powerful as to preclude the necessity of the entire procedure.

1. I imagine myself on my deathbed, someday off in the future. I get outside the immediate situation, project myself into history, and see myself, in fantasy, lying on my bed, about to die. What decision would I like to have made, way back then when I made it? Such a fantasy, lived with for one or several periods of prayer, sometimes provides perspective on a decision that renders it immediately clear in terms of my deepest values, my best and truest self.

2. Similarly, I place myself before the judgment seat of God. My life is over and I am meeting with the God who

loves me to evaluate my life. Before the eyes of God what would I like to have decided? This is a possibly freeing question.

3. I imagine someone I love coming to talk with me. This person trusts me very much and asks me the same question I am asking. How would I direct this other person? What advice would I give to another in the same situation as myself? Perhaps this objectification will shed light on my own decision.

When the decision to be made is more complex, when more time is available, and more certainty is desired, the director may invite me to make the most careful, prayerful decision possible. The following are steps of such a process.

1. *Gather the necessary data:* Before trying to pray over a decision facing me I need to be sure I have whatever I can have as information aiding a wise decision. I may want to get a personality study or take an aptitude test. I may need to ask some significant others in my life what effects my decision will have on them. I may need to talk with experts in one field or another to shed light on a subject of which I am relatively ignorant.

2. *Consider the negative side:* When I have the needed information, I take a period of time to look separately at each side of the question. I take the negative side first. That can be confusing. The negative side is not always clear, but (if possible to decide) I first pick that side which seems less attractive. For example, considering a vocation change, I would initially focus on the situation I am already in. If a question had not arisen that attracted me elsewhere, I would not be considering the change, so I first take the apparently negative situation in which I exist. If I am going to pray about whether or not to get married, I would first take the single life I am in, for something (or someone) seems to be calling me, positively, out of that state. This is admittedly not always clear, and it does not matter greatly which I consider first. The main thing is to consider only one side.

For a specific period, depending on how much time I have to decide, and how important the decision may be, I avoid going around in circles and arguing with myself. I simply go before God and ask for help, listening to my own heart, listening to everything I can in the readings of Scripture for each day, in the voices of others, and in the movements and moods of my life. At the end of each day, I write down every supporting reason for the side I am considering. I make the most comprehensive list possible. I weigh the relative importance of each reason and bring the decision to Mass with me, offering it to God. I look at this one side for several days, carefully noticing how I feel for the entire time I have allotted.

3. *Take the positive side:* Then for the same period of time, I consider only the other alternative, the positive reasons for making this choice. I take the same procedure: I listen to my feelings, compile a list, offer my reflections to God, ask for guidance, and listen for it.

4. *Make a tentative choice:* At the end of this period of time, I look at my two lists, recall my feelings, weigh the information I have received as best I can, and then make a tentative choice. The final choice is not actually made, but I have decided to make it and live with the decision for a while before committing myself to it. I pay attention to feelings, look for peace. Can I live with this decision? Does it seem right and good? When I offer it to God, does it seem accepted? When I listen to the Scripture readings at Mass, or sit with them in my own private prayer, does anything confirm me in this decision? Almost invariably at this stage I will experience profound peace and a deep sense of being "on the right track."

5. *Make the decision:* If I do experience peace in the previous stage, I can now make the decision knowing that I did the best I could to listen, and I can refuse to look back over my shoulder, feeling guilty about the negative factors which are necessarily a part of any significant human decision. I did the best I could, with God's help. I am at peace. I decide.

6. *If there is no peace* during the tentative decision stage, I simply back up a step, and tentatively make the alternate decision. Perhaps the first was more reasonable and seemed right, but I simply could not live with it. I try the other choice, applying the same procedure, listening to God, noticing my

feelings, and testing out the "rightness" of this other side. If peace is arrived at this time, this is the decision. I make it, trust it, and do not look back.

7. *If I do not experience peace* in either case, I can follow one of two routes. I can postpone the decision, if that is possible. I simply am not ready to make it now, at least peacefully and out of prayer. If I cannot postpone the decision any longer, I will flip a coin and trust in God. There is no clear answer and any decision is all right. Like the eleven apostles picking a successor to Judas, I can simply draw straws and trust that I did the best I could to let the Lord lead me.

Almost invariably the decision will be made upon completion of the initial process (step 5). Only rarely will the process end without a clear decision.

The director is significant all the way through, both suggesting the process and monitoring its steps. The director listens, suggests things not thought of, acts as a sounding board, helps another pay close attention to feelings, and, generally, supports through a difficult time. The director also serves as an accountability factor, whose continued presence almost forces people to deal with something they would rather avoid. Most importantly, the director provides that divine sense to people that they will be loved no matter what they finally decide, a provision that makes the entire process incarnational, credible, and grace-filled.

Finally, a word on the *peace* that we seek. It is difficult to describe. It definitely is not the superficial peace of relief that the choice has been made. Right or wrong, it is human to feel better when something is "off our back." That is not the peace we mean. What we aim at is that deep-down peace, that sense of the Holy Spirit, that I am indeed in touch with the Lord who lives in me. I know that God loves me, and I know it more deeply when I stand with this decision and say "yes." It is the peace of coming home.

Naturally, we will guide another through this process most aptly if we have experienced it personally and thus believe in it profoundly. Even without this experience, guiding another through it once or twice will help us to believe that God can lead and guide if we open ourselves to that loving power.

NOTE

1. For a readable treatment of this material, see David L. Fleming, S.J., *A Contemporary Reading of the Spiritual Exercises of St. Ignatius* (St. Louis: Institute of Jesuit Sources, 1976), pp. 51-57.

9 MYSTICS AND PROPHETS

Among Catholics, the chaotic currents of change set in motion by Vatican II seem to have settled into a number of fairly obvious channels. There is on the one hand the stream of individual renewal and spiritual growth. Its manifestations range from the charismatic movement to marriage encounter, from the search for spiritual direction or guidance in prayer to the building of satisfying liturgical community. Some of these movements certainly extend beyond the limits of personal spirituality; but insofar as they are directed principally to the inner needs of individual Christians or Christian groups, they represent a truncated expression of Christian spirituality.

On the other hand, there is a growing emphasis on social justice and the radical demands of a Christian lifestyle in a world of limited resources and a country whose affluence depends on depriving much of the rest of the world of a share of the good things of creation. Political activists and lobbyists, families trying to live simply, alternative communities, revolutionaries are all part of this stream. Where their efforts are not grounded in prayer and centered on love of God through love of neighbor, they too represent a truncated spirituality.

The challenge facing Catholics and all Christians today is to rediscover a spirituality that lives and prays justly, that unites flesh and spirit, that celebrates life even as it confronts the powers of death and destruction in the world and in ourselves. This new yet old spirituality is ecumenical in the most profound sense: reconciling and uniting sisters and brothers everywhere, and so extending the body of Christ throughout the oikumene*—the whole world. To live this spirituality is to actively expect the resurrection, to look forward to the restoration of all creation, and to celebrate and share that future hope now in the Eucharist, the sacrament of the new community that exists not for itself but for the world and for God.*[1]

We Christians wake up every morning schizophrenic. On the one hand life is so lovely, so undeserved, so precious. God is so loving. Beauty and laughter surround us. It is good to be alive, good to be held in the palm of the hand of a loving God. There is so much to celebrate in life.

On the other hand, so much remains unfinished, so much unredeemed, with so much suffering and pain within and around us. Celebration and struggle are apparent opposites and yet necessary parts of integrated Christian life.

Here in the northwestern part of our country, the mountains and water, trees and hills are lovely. Here, as anywhere, we relish the gifts of intimacy in friendship and bonding in community. At the same time twenty thousand people in Seattle are homeless every night. Fifty million people in our world are starving every day. How do we hold the tension of this awareness together?

Some of us manage to get through life drinking beer and watching football games on TV. But if we enter into the struggles of the world, three things can happen. We can join with people in their fears and sorrows, face head-on the violence in our societies, and become bitter, angry, and cynical. We can take up a rock, a club, or a gun and add to the violence. Though understandable, especially in some cases, this approach is questionably Christian and chooses only one side of the tension.

Or we can join in the struggles and hopes of others and become deeply pained, withdraw with a few like-minded people to a hillside or a church, and celebrate our lives together, forgetting the less joyful lives of those outside our chosen circle. While we praise the Lord, we are removing ourselves from his incarnational presence and choosing one side of the tension, seeing only the joy.

The balanced Christian enters into the very real world of which we are a part, seeing the pain and anguish there, and not denying it, but struggling to alleviate it. Yet at the same time and in the same place, we celebrate the life that is there too, see the beauty, accept the love, and constantly hope for the fulfillment of the promise that is present. Our task is to hold the tension together, denying neither side of it. Put in other words, our Christian call is to rejoice in the constant, mystical presence of God in people, in events, in myself, in the whole of the world; yet, at the same time, we speak, in some fashion, a prophetic word to that world where it is not yet fully redeemed.

The question then becomes: How do we continue to pray, letting God love us, and at the same time struggle for justice? God invites each of us to be intimately united with him in prayerful contemplation of how loved we are, and, at the same time, to be moved by that love to enter into the Lord's work of building God's kingdom of justice, love, and peace.

We judge authentic spirituality ultimately by how well we are able to keep the paradox alive. As spiritual directors, we hope to enable others to keep the tension from evaporating.

This entire book treats spirituality, but only now at the end do we attempt to define our subject. Hopefully, every page has helped to shape this definition:

SPIRITUALITY IS THE STYLE OF A
PERSON'S RESPONSE TO CHRIST
BEFORE THE CHALLENGE OF EVERYDAY LIFE,
IN A GIVEN HISTORICAL
AND CULTURAL ENVIRONMENT.

It is in the here and now of our individual personality, history, and environment that we hear the call to be mystic—to experience God's loving presence, to live more and more by faith. To be mystic, "contemplative," means simply that we have a growing but unconscious (or unselfconscious) awareness of the reality of God and our oneness with him.

We all have moments, touches, experiences of God, immediate and direct, usually unsought for. We all have "mystic" experiences. We are moved, momentarily at least, by the absolute loveliness of a mountain peak, or the sun setting over the ocean, or the incredible gift of friendship. We are awed at the loveliness of a child, a poem, a painting. We all have at least fleeting glimpses of the benignity at the heart of the universe, the sense of meaning, the ultimate graciousness of life. Not all live, work, and pray within a milieu that supports and sustains such experiences. Not all take the time to remember those graced moments or to foster new and deeper ones, and so to trust them and build a life upon them. We exist in different frameworks, theologies, life-styles, language sets, but all, it seems to us, are invited into such experiences. All are called to be mystics.

In fact, one very real way of viewing the Church and every community within the Church is as those places where such visions are built up, such experiences are fostered. Within the ecclesial community we learn to trust and to build our lives of faith upon our shared touches of the Almighty.

For some of us the starting point for a mystic life is the goodness or the needs of people, which will lead us into prayer, reflection, and deeper awareness of the reality before us. Others, centered in a profound prayer relationship, a union with God, are thereby impelled into the lives of people, into the challenge of entering life more fully.

The two of us differ profoundly in this area. Katherine, would, in germ at least, be very happy to pray often and deeply, and let much of the world go by, but God continues to call her out of herself in service to others. Pat would perhaps never pray except that his dealing with people constantly drives him into searching for meaning and hope. The starting point is not as important as that the circle be complete: prayer leading to life, and life leading to prayer. Real prayer leads to involvement; real involvement leads to prayer. Deeper spirituality impels to action; action impels to deeper spirituality, and the circle continues and deepens. The mystic becomes prophet, the prophet becomes mystic.

As spiritual directors we work with people grounded, to some extent at least, in the same faith stance as ourselves. We share some commonality of language. We can enable others to see the relationship between their experiences of God and the needs around them, and then see the relationship between the needs around them and their own relationship with God.

In the first chapter we spoke at length about the growth

of faith, the dynamic that people commonly go through as faith deepens. We spoke of *conversion, struggle,* a deepening sense of *integrity,* of *reality,* and, ultimately, of *radicality.* These elements are discovered in the lives of all the historically prominent mystics and in the lives of people around us. The person deepening in prayer and growing in faith is not called *out* of the world to be with God, but is more profoundly immersed *in* that world's heart.

We think of Ignatius of Loyola deliberately having to put aside his visions of the Trinity in order to learn to conjugate the Latin verb amo (I love). He put aside visions so that he could finish school, be ordained, and serve God and God's people.

We think of Thomas Merton putting aside his own desire to be a hermit in order to continue the arduous task of studying, writing, and translating that his superiors gave him. At the same time, he suffered the misunderstanding of his fellow monks who thought him too involved in the works of the world.

The great mystics were not people who withdrew, hid, found God in solitude and stayed there. We may become more passive in prayer, but that does not mean becoming passive in life. St. John of the Cross founded a college of which he was for many years the rector. Because of the reforms he initiated, he was imprisoned by his own men for a number of months. It was during this time that he composed some of his greatest writings. His mystic companion, Teresa of Avila, was not in some ivory tower feeling good with Jesus. In fact, out of her own darkness of many years, she remained balanced and witty, founded several new monasteries, and reformed her entire congregation. She found time to advise many priests and to do a great deal of writing. Somehow the great heroes of prayer became great because their prayer immersed them in life.

How misled we have been by hagiographers. We think of the stories of St. Aloysius who kept the rules perfectly and seems to have been canonized because he was so pious. But he died helping the victims of the plague in the streets of Rome, laying down his life for his friends. We distort the picture of holiness if we divorce it from the prophetic dimension to which it always leads.

In our own day, Jean Vanier touches the wounds of Jesus and experiences his own weakness, but travels the world setting up a network of places for people, wounded people, to be together, and therefore strong. He preaches many retreats but always in the context of our need to be samaritans to one another. Mother Teresa of Calcutta is touched by God and leaves her beloved community to begin a new one and care for dying people on the streets of Calcutta and (perhaps more importantly) to challenge every aspect of the life style of the rest of us.

All these holy people are holy not just because they pray or write eloquently about that prayer, but because their prayer leads them to respond to Christ in the given historical cultural moment. All of them respond in a unique way to unique situations in which they find the Lord calling to his people. But all respond outside themselves in service. Each mystic becomes a prophet.

We do not need to go to the great and famous. We all know people within our experience who have been touched by God, have acknowledged that touch, and have let it lead them into new ways of being with their God incarnate in the histories of people.

We think of a woman suddenly widowed who out of her own grief creates a new ministry to dying patients and their families. We know doctors suddenly driven to their knees by some personal tragedy who discover new life working in a ghetto health clinic. We know an aging priest-administrator, threatened by the loss of his eyesight, who discovers a new ability to minister to the shut-in, sick, and lonely people around him. We know a family who sells its expensive home by the lake and moves into the inner city to work with a parish struggling to return to life. We know a sister who found herself initially so disturbed by renewal within her community that she doubted her own vocation, but soon found herself out of the classroom with a whole new personal ministry to the street people of the Seattle waterfront.

Over and over again, we praying people are converted, struggle, become more integrated, more realistic, and more radicalized as prayer leads us into the mission and ministry of Jesus. Over and over the story of God discovered in the depths of our lives calls us to new vibrancy, new vision, new mission.

And so as we direct others in their journey, humbled by the experience, we see the mystic call and the prophetic call coming together. The beauty of God's love and God's activity in the world are profoundly realized; the invitation to celebrate this beauty is equally intense. This intensity is coupled with the deepening desire to mend what is unfinished in this broken world, at least in that part that touches and calls to us. In us, as we grow in relationship with God, there will be a new call to some kind of action, some new voice of radicality, striking at the heart of what is not yet redeemed.

We as directors need to know that prayer eventually always invites us to become, in our own unique way, in our history and culture, a prophet. It is apparently possible for piety and social intransigence to walk hand in hand to church every day, but authentic spirituality is not piety. It does not remove us from the world but immerses us more deeply in it. Authentic spirituality will always include some uprooting and rerooting. "I come not to bring peace but the sword" (Mt. 10:34) forms a necessary part of the Savior's voice in our listening hearts. Justice is the prophet's goal. Prayer in some form will always become a critique of ideologies, putting into question what is, in the presence of a vision of what might be, a vision of justice.

The world has too many uncritical lovers, too many unloving critics. What we need and hunger for are critical lovers, those who love the world intensely, as Jesus did, and so criticize it and try to correct it, as Jesus did. The radicality may not arise in areas that another would predict, but one way or another, in some part or another, the prayerful person will assume the prophetic stance.

In *On Becoming a Musical, Mystical Bear,* Matthew Fox indicates the signs of an authentic prophet.[2] We repeat and comment on those points here as signs of authentic prayer. As directors we look for and foster these signs which are as important as the inter- or intra-personal signs we indicated in a previous chapter.

PERSONAL REROOTING

There will be some personal rerooting, specifically in Jesus and his love for life. We will be converted in favor of life. We will become a radical lover, not a fanatic. And so that older priest, threatened with blindness, begins to see the beauty of aging people around him. He treasures what is rich and deep in their experience, their past, and thus knows how valuable their futures can be. He cannot but help them to see that value and be eager to share it with them.

RELUCTANCE

The praying prophet will be a reluctant prophet. Although deeply convinced of a wrong that must be made right, we are shy to speak out. We do not act on our own but are urged by another, urged by the love of Christ. We are deeply aware that whatever we say or do is addressed first and foremost to ourselves. It is here that the authentic prophet is distinguished from another angry voice. Jeremiah did not want to speak doom to Israel; Moses did not want to confront the Pharaoh. Driven by an inner voice, they could not say "no." The simple priest, the responsible mother and wife, and the sister teaching first grade do not want to climb the fence of that nuclear submarine base and speak out with their own lives against nuclear armament, but they can no longer remain silent, for their own sakes as well as for ours.

CREATIVITY

The prayerful prophet will be creative. We attempt to build life again into what has become dull or ancient. We discover new ways to address an issue and encourage others to this newness. One senses the freshness of the Spirit of God. Thus Jean Vanier begins an entirely new social movement, a fresh way of caring for the wounded (and the "healthy") of our society. And the older, wiser, prayerful pastor continually encourages the new approaches of his assistant in things that would never have occurred to him.

COMMUNITY ORIENTATION

And because our prayer is not private, nor limited, but includes the whole of God's kingdom, the prophetic voice develops an ever wider community orientation, a sense of consciousness of and commitment to human solidarity, a sense of our global village. Concern revolves not simply around what will satisfy us, or our smaller community's needs for warmth, kindness and success. And so the principal of a school, deeply concerned with its financial survival, also sees that the selling of chocolate bars is a humanly destructive way to raise money. She decides on a jog-a-thon instead as more productive human growth and better modeling, not just to her students but to all who contribute to them. A parish leader sees that although the school playground is valuable, a part of it could be better used as a site for a retirement home for the growing number of elderly in the neighborhood, and such a sacrifice would be good even for the children involved.

WILLINGNESS TO PAY THE PRICE

Finally, the authentic prayerful prophet is willing to pay the price. We know that to speak on this issue, to take this stand, to say "no" at this juncture, will bring misunderstanding, rebuke, and the cross. From time to time only hope provides a sustaining power, our ultimate hope in the God who loves us and called us to this place. And so the popular young parish priest forsakes that popularity and is arrested in a stand against nuclear arms. The concerned mother speaks out against racism in the local parish school. The parish council continues to involve women extensively in ministry as the collections go down. Love will bring suffering, even to others, but the prayerful person knows that the only real evil is sin, not pain, and continues to speak, to act.

All of us Christians, not just some "specially chosen," are called to be deeply united to God in prayer and to speak out of that prayer with some strand of prophetic voice. Everyone is called to be both mystic and prophet. In our direction of others, we are called to encourage, support, sustain, and challenge our fellow believers into that fullness of God's message and mission while attempting to realize the same in ourselves. We have the glorious opportunity of ministering to God's people, inviting them to the mystic relationship, and supporting in them the prophetic voice that is our common call in Christ.

NOTES

1. Francine Cardman, "A Lightning Look at the History of Christian Spirituality," in *The Wind Is Rising* (Washington, D.C.: Quixote Center, 1978), p. 40.
2. Matthew Fox, O.P., *On Becoming a Musical, Mystical Bear*, pp. 109–116.

APPENDIX

> *Glory be to him whose power working in us can do infinitely more than we can ask or imagine. Glory be to him forever in the Church, and in Christ Jesus. Amen (Eph. 3:20–21).*

Though we have written the chapters and sections of this book with titles and sub-headings, this is imprecise. Human beings are one, and yet complex. They cannot be divided into parts (now we are mystics, now prophets; now we are counselors, now spiritual directors; now we are talking about prayer, now about life, etc.). We are one, and we do not experience things neatly in packages. The information at the end of the last chapter may be a more helpful starting point than the first chapter. The process for leading one in prayerful decision making may never occur in your particular relationship, or it may provide the starting point. The experience of the desert may come in the midst of a mid-life crisis or already have been passed in young adulthood. The charts cannot be neatly laid out like the course of a predictable train. The director has a sense of the whole, a trust in God, and deals with the parts as they come, however they may come.

Throughout the entire book, we have been trying to define what we mean by spiritual direction. In a book on the practice of contemplative prayer in groups, *Pilgrimage Home,* Gerald May invites several people to describe what they believe a spiritual director should be. Their responses touch upon many of the things we have already described. Listen to some of them.[1]

> "Be a theologian, i.e., one who doesn't get trapped by any foreign environment; have a sense of one's own personal and religious institutional history, seeing their pilgrim relativity and the more basic gift of peace."

"Have experienced a movement from despair to grace, have a spirit of prayer, common sense, and intelligence."

"Be over 35 years old."

" . . . have gotten through messianism."

"Have an applied knowledge of both psychological and spirituality areas."

" . . . hospitality; openness, an ability to welcome all of life."

"Do oneself out of business."

"Have a loving patience."

"Have the capacity to step aside and let the Spirit of Christ do the direction—skill development is secondary to this."

"Have a detached compassion, not needing the relationship; also gifts of the Spirit and a radical self-giving to the Lord."

"Be in full communion with the whole of your humanity—not airy-fairy; be in the body of some tradition where there can be external validation of your experience."

"Capacity to notice movement of the Spirit and to provide an environment out of which a person can pay attention and allow this intuitive noticing to become an important part of his/her life."

"Be a fellow searcher."

The task that these definitions imply, and our entire presentation specifies, becomes almost overwhelming. A few words of consolation and encouragment are needed.

We may have a constant temptation to say that we are not the ones for the job. Others are more profound, more experienced, more astute, and, especially, holier than we. They ought to be the directors of others. This recognition, rather than driving us away from the task, is precisely the insight that will help make us adequate spiritual directors. It will lead us to deep dependence on God, based on the realization that God, the Holy Spirit, leads us all. There are not better people around for the task—only sinners, fragile people like ourselves.

What we are invited to do as directors is to be open in sharing our own growing faith in God, our own journey, our own struggles, and to be with others in theirs. We can grow continually in our understandings of the way God seems to work. We can increase our comprehension of Scripture and our ability to suggest various passages that seem to fit particular life situations. We can deepen our awareness of psychology and our understanding of the human person. We can develop more techniques in prayer to suggest to people. We can and should read, study, and pray more. All of these will make us better instruments of the Lord's work. But we cannot wait until we are *ready* to begin or we will *never* be ready, *never* will begin. The very doing of the work will call us to deepen our ability to do it, and our dependence on God will deepen our success with it.

NOTE

1. Gerald G. May, *Pilgrimage Home* (New York; Paulist Press, 1979), pp. 158–159.

SELECTED BIBLIOGRAPHY

Abbott, Walter M., S.J., ed. *The Documents of Vatican II.* New York: Guild Press, 1966.

Abhishiktananda (Fr. Henri Le Saux, O.S.B.), *Prayer.* Philadelphia: Westminster Press, 1972.

Bailey, Raymond. *Thomas Merton on Mysticism.* New York: Image Books, 1975.

Bloom, Anthony. *Beginning To Pray.* New York: Paulist Press, 1970.

Callahan, William, S.J., and Francine Cardman. *The Wind Is Rising.* Washington, D.C.: Quixote Center, 1978.

Carlson, Gregory, S.J. "Spiritual Direction and the Paschal Mystery." *Review for Religious,* May 1974, pp. 532–541.

Carroll, L. Patrick, S.J. *To Love, To Share, To Serve: Challenges to a Religious.* Collegeville: Liturgical Press, 1979.

Connolly, William, S.J. "Noticing Key Interior Facts in the Early Stage of Spiritual Direction." *Review for Religious,* January 1976, pp. 112–121.

Cummings, Charles. *Spirituality and the Desert Experience.* Denville, N.J.: Dimension Books, 1978.

De Mello, Anthony, S.J. *Sadhana.* St. Louis: Institute of Jesuit Sources, 1978.

English, John, S.J. *Spiritual Freedom.* Guelph, Ontario: Loyola House, 1973.

Farrell, Edward. *Prayer Is a Hunger.* Denville, N.J.: Dimension Books, 1972.

Finley, James. *Merton's Palace of Nowhere.* Notre Dame: Ave Maria Press, 1978.

Fleming David L., S.J. *A Contemporary Reading of the Spiritual Exercises of St. Ignatius.* St. Louis: Institute of Jesuit Sources, 1976.

Fowler, James and Sam Keen. *Life Maps: Conversations on the Journey of Faith.* Waco, Texas: Word Books, 1978.

Fox, Matthew, O.P. *On Becoming a Musical, Mystical Bear.* New York: Paulist Press, 1976.

Futrell, John, S.J. "Ignatian Discernment." *Studies in the Spirituality of Jesuits,* II (April 1970).

Ginn, Roman, O.C.S.O. *Adventure in Spiritual Direction.* Locust Valley, N.Y.: Living Flame Press, 1979.

Gould, Roger. "The Phases in Adult Life: A Study in Developmental Psychology." *American Journal of Psychiatry,* 129 (1972), pp. 33–43.

Gray, Howard, S.J. "Giving Form to Vision Through Spiritual Direction." National Sisters' Vocation Conference, 1307 So. Wabash Ave., Chicago, Ill., 60605.

Green, Thomas. *When the Well Runs Dry.* Notre Dame: Ave Maria Press, 1979.

Hocken, P. *Prayer, Gift of Life.* New York: Paulist Press, 1974.

John of the Cross. *The Collected Works of St. John of the Cross.* Translated by Kieran Kavanaugh, O.C.D. and Otilio Rodriguez, O.C.D. Washington, D.C.: ICS Publications, 1973.

Johnston, William S.J. *Silent Music: The Science of Meditation.* New York: Harper and Row, 1974.

———. *The Inner Eye of Love.* San Francisco: Harper and Row, 1978.

Jung, C. J. *Man and His Symbols.* New York: Doubleday, 1964.

———. *Psyche and Symbol.* Edited by Violet S. de Laszlo. New York: Doubleday and Co., 1958.

Kelsey, Morton. *The Other Side of Silence.* New York: Paulist Press, 1976.

Kopp, Sheldon B., *If You Meet the Buddha on the Road, Kill Him!* New York: Bantam Books, 1979.

LaPlace, Jean, S.J. *Preparing for Spiritual Direction.* Chicago: Franciscan Herald Press, 1975.

Leech, Kenneth. *Soul Friend.* San Francisco: Harper and Row, 1977.

———. *True Prayer.* London: Sheldon Press, 1980.

Levinson, Daniel. *The Seasons of a Man's Life.* New York: Knopf, 1978.

McCarty, Shaun, S.T. "On Entering Spiritual Direction." *Review for Religious,* November 1976, pp. 854–867.

McNamara, William O.C.D. *Mystical Passion: Spirituality for a Bored Society.* New York: Paulist Press, 1977.

Maloney, George, S.J. *The Breath of the Mystic.* Denville, N.J.: Dimension Books, 1974.

———. *Inward Stillness.* Denville, N.J.: Dimension Books, 1976.

May, Gerald G. *Pigrimage Home.* New York: Paulist Press, 1979.

Merton, Thomas. *Spiritual Direction and Meditation.* Collegevillle: Liturgical Press, 1960.

———. *New Seeds of Contemplation.* New York: New Directions, 1961.

———. "The Spiritual Father in the Desert Tradition." *Cistercian Studies,* 3:1(1968), pp. 3–23.

———. *Contemplation in a World of Action.* New York: Doubleday and Co., 1971.

Nouwen, Henri. *The Wounded Healer.* New York: Image Books, 1979.

———. *Reaching Out: The Three Movements of the Spiritual Life.* New York: Doubleday, 1975.

———. *Clowning in Rome.* New York: Image Books, 1979.

Pennington, Basil M. *Daily We Touch Him.* New York: Image Books, 1979.

———. *Centering Prayer.* New York: Doubleday and Co., 1980.

Sanford, John A. *Healing and Wholeness.* New York: Paulist Press, 1977.

Schneiders, Sandra. "The Contemporary Ministry of Spiritual Direction." *Chicago Studies,* Spring 1976, pp. 119–135.

Shea, John. *Stories of God.* Chicago: The Thomas More Press, 1978.

Smith, John. *The Bush Still Burns.* Kansas City: Sheed, Andrews and McMeel, Inc., 1978.

Tillich, Paul. *Dynamics of Faith.* New York: Harper and Row, 1957.

Topel, John, S.J. *The Way to Peace: Liberation Through the Bible.* New York: Orbis Books, 1979.

Whitehead, Evelyn E. and James D. Whitehead. *Christian Life Patterns.* New York: Doubleday and Co., 1979.

Wright, John H., S.J. "Two Discussions: On Spiritual Direction and On Leadership and Authority" *Studies in the Spirituality of Jesuits,* IV (March 1972).